TITLE DESIGN
ESSENTIALS

for Film and Video

Mary Plummer

Title Design Essentials for Film and Video
Mary Plummer

Peachpit Press
1249 Eighth Street
Berkeley, CA 94710
510/524-2178
800/283-9444
510/524-2221 (fax)

Find us on the Web at: www.peachpit.com
To report errors, please send a note to errata@peachpit.com

Peachpit Press is a division of Pearson Education

Project Editor: Rebecca Gulick
Editor: Anne Marie Walker
Production Editor: Hilal Sala
Technical Editor: Klark Perez
Interior Designer and Compositor: Kim Scott, Bumpy Design
Media Reviewer: Eric Geoffroy
Indexer: Rebecca Plunkett
Cover Designer: Charlene Will

Notice of Rights

Notice of Liability

Trademarks

Acknowledgments

First and foremost, deepest heartfelt thanks to my husband and partner in business and life, Klark Perez, for your incredible devotion and strength in carrying the weight for both of us and our company, InVision Digital and Media Arts, while I was writing. You helped juggle everything—from our new baby to training to my crazy writing schedule—without missing a beat, and you still found room to take on more with a smile.

Thanks to Marjorie Baer for the idea, inspiration, and opportunity to write this book. Also thanks to Victor Gavenda and Camille Peri for your kindness and endurance during my postpartum writing schedule and lack thereof.

Special thanks to Anne Marie Walker for your patience, valued input, and attention to detail with every element of this book. Also thanks to Rebecca Gulick for your guidance and care in honing the direction of this writing adventure. Extra special thanks to the entire Peachpit team for all of your efforts on this truly unique book.

Thanks to Patty Montesion for giving me my first industry book writing assignment and for your continued support in a career I adore. Also thanks to our friends at Universal Studios Florida for the opportunity to have a production company and training center on the lot.

Infinite thanks to my family members for their unconditional love throughout my freelance career. Thanks Mom "Meem," Lee, Dad, Ginny, Chris, Sessely, Jorin, Landon, Kim, Guy, Emily, Chris, Jackson, Gabe, Warren, Loretta, Chase, Bill, Paula, Peg, Jim, Sergio, Virginia, Kent, Klark, our baby Katie who inspires me daily, and my dog Niki.

Contents

Introduction

One thing all video projects have in common is titles. Large or small, wordy or succinct, plentiful or few, a project's titles support its identity and message. Effective titles are memorable, legible, and convey specific information in a finite amount of time. On the other hand, ineffective titles are difficult to read—let alone remember—and leave the viewer confused, distracted, or worse, lose the viewer's attention altogether.

The concept of creating titles is simple: Add text to your project. It's the details of the text that separate professional-looking titles from all the rest.

So who is responsible for creating titles anyway? Years ago, titles were carefully crafted by graphic designers and titling artist. However, with the advent of the personal computer and professional editing software the job now falls to the video editor. Sure, there are still graphic design teams out there creating beautiful titles. But often, it's the video editor who must create and apply the titles to finish a project.

Chances are, if you're reading this introduction, you are a video editor or motion graphics designer by choice, or by default, and are looking to hone your titling skills. Well, you've come to the right place. This book will help you understand the essential elements of video title design from the font selection to text placement and choreographing animation.

The Book's Structure

Each chapter of the book builds on the skills explained in the previous chapter, not only giving you hands-on titling experience, but also strengthening your title design foundation to apply to your own projects. You can either start at the beginning of the book and work through it sequentially or jump around to the pertinent sections as needed.

Along the way you'll learn tips, tricks, and troubleshooting for common titling issues. You'll also see over 100 examples to illustrate different titling variations as well as spark your imagination.

Software Requirements

Most professional editing and graphics design applications include tools for creating and enhancing text. Before you begin, you should have a basic understanding of your software, such as starting a new project, importing a QuickTime file, and creating a basic title.

The exercises you'll work on throughout the book were created in a variety of applications, such as Photoshop, LiveType, Motion, Final Cut Pro, or After Effects. These titling techniques aren't designed to teach you specific software; instead, they demonstrate how to apply different software tools and features to enhance your own titling projects with the applications that you have available to you.

CHAPTER 1

Creating Effective Basic Titles

W hether you're a seasoned professional or just starting out, you'll find everything you need in this section to serve up tasteful and effective basic titles.

Before you create exciting animated titles, it's a good idea to understand the title fundamentals and additional elements that make up or enhance basic titles. Once you know how to create solid and effective basic titles, making them move, fade, flash, or animate is just icing on the cake. However, if you don't have functional titles to start with, animation and frills aren't going to make them any more effective.

Think of basic titles as an ordinary cake: If the cake is good, people will eat it and enjoy it regardless of its fundamental ingredients. On the other hand, if the cake is lousy, missing key ingredients, or tastes awful, it's unlikely that adding more icing and decorations will improve it. Sometimes a simple cake is all that's desired, just like basic titles may be all that are needed for a particular project. Icing alone doesn't make much of a dessert, and too much icing can be a real turn off.

This chapter focuses on understanding the purpose of your titles and title categories, and selecting appropriate fonts, sizes, styles, and text placement to achieve your goal. Once the text is created and in place, you'll work with additional features such as drop shadow, outline, and color to enhance your basic titles against the background.

Basic Title Categories

Different types of text make up the titles of a project. These different title categories apply to a wide range of projects, from feature films to television commercials, training videos, streaming video, and podcasts.

NOTE: The text examples in the "Basic Title Categories" section follow many of the basic rules of title design that will be discussed in detail throughout this chapter.

Main title is the name of the show, or project, and often sets the tone visually for the entire piece.

Credits are exactly what they sound like, an acknowledgment of credit for participation in a project. Credits can be displayed as scrolling text acknowledging hundreds of names or as title cards acknowledging one or two individuals at a time.

Single title card   *Double title card*   *Scrolling credits*

Lower third is text placed over a picture to identify a person, place, time, or thing and is usually located in the lower third of the screen. In addition to text, lower thirds also include graphics, lines, blurs, or composites to separate the text from the underlying picture.

Key information text includes dates, times, and contact information, such as a phone number, address, or Web site.

<table>
<tr><td>555-323-4567</td><td>May 15, 2006</td><td>2000 Universal Studios Plaza
Suite 602
Orlando, FL 32819</td></tr>
</table>

Lists are points listed numerically, using bullets, dashes, or other punctuation.

INGREDIENTS

1 Can of Juice
3 Cups of Lime Soda
2 Cups of Frozen Fruit
3 Tbs Sugar
5 Oz Citris Extract

CUSTOMER BENEFITS

• Better Service
• Higher Quality
• Bigger Savings
• Taller Building
• Smaller Lines

Entering Room

1. Open the door
2. Step through the doorway
3. Turn to door
4. Grasp door knob
5. Pull door closed

Text blocks are paragraphs of text, such as a prologue to a movie, or fine-print disclaimer paragraphs commonly seen in commercials.

Movie prologue text block

Product disclaimer fine-print text block

Interjections WOW! Huge Sale! Today Only!!! Don't Pay Too Much! Top Quality! Like the part of speech with the same name, interjections are text words or phrases used in commercials and sales videos to express strong emotion or feelings.

Crawl Crawling text generally appears at the very top or bottom of the screen and contains information such as stock reports, sports results, weather updates, and additional news stories.

Intellectual property rights text includes the copyright, trademark, publishing, or patent information.

Watermarks include text or logos that are embedded into the picture as a means of identification, branding, or copy protection.

Understanding Titling Goals

The secret to creating effective titles is to understand the purpose of your titles and make design decisions that support your goals. Sure, that sounds easy. Yet, I've witnessed many editors and novice title designers who stray from their original title plans while exploring other nifty title fonts and features.

Your title plan can require skills as complex and design-demanding as capturing the look and feel of your project for the main title or as simple as displaying the phone number and date of a charity event.

As you work through the different titling techniques in this book, you'll often be reminded of your goals to keep your titles on track and make sure they serve their purpose and are as effective as possible.

Choosing Fonts and Styling Text

Choosing a font or font family can be a daunting process considering the thousands of fonts from which to choose. This chapter helps you understand the different types of fonts and styles, so you can sift through them and choose one that will enhance your project rather than detract from it.

Font is the technical name for a set of type characters that includes the full alphabet in uppercase and lowercase plus its associated punctuation and numbers with the same design and size.

Fonts are sorted into six primary categories: symbol fonts, decorative fonts, script fonts, antique fonts, serifed fonts, and sans serif fonts.

Symbol fonts are created with graphic icons instead of alphabetical letters and numbers, and are designed to decorate or embellish text.

Decorative fonts are decorated, exotic, ornate, or eccentric and are often used for company logos, main titles, and credits, but are rarely used in sentences, key information, or blocks of text.

Script fonts are designed to represent handwriting, either printed or scripted, using a variety of writing instruments from chalk to a quill pen. These fonts are most often used for main titles and credits to capture the style and feel of a project.

Antique fonts have a historic feel and add an authentic, historical, or period look to the text. These fonts are also used primarily in main titles and credits to reflect the overall style or time period of a project.

ABCDEFGhijklmnopQRSTUVWXYZ

Serifed fonts are designed for easy, fluid reading and legibility. These fonts are often referred to as book fonts and are ideal for large amounts of text. *Serifs* are the details at the beginning and end of a stroke when drawing letterforms, and appear as horizontal, vertical, or diagonal lines that slightly extend from the strokes for each character. Serifed fonts are used in all of the title categories, especially text blocks, lower thirds, intellectual property rights, and credits.

ABCDEFGhijklmnopqrstuVWXYZ

Sans serif fonts are fonts without serifs, presenting a more modern, clean look. They are used in all of the different title categories, most commonly credits, text blocks, crawling text, and lower thirds.

ABCDEFGhijklmnopQRSTUVWXYZ

Adding Personality to Your Titles

The font or fonts that you choose for a project's titles should reflect the personality or context of the project. For example, if you compare a danger high voltage sign to a traditional wedding invitation, you'd clearly see that the high voltage sign uses big, bold, capital letters to catch your attention as if screaming DANGER, whereas the letters in the wedding invitation are light and delicately scripted or italicized to suggest a quiet, intimate, and beautiful event.

The same theory goes for video titles. An action or disaster movie uses a large, bold font to suggest action or danger, whereas a traditional wedding video uses a scripted or italicized font for the main titles.

Whichever computer platform or application you may be using, take the time to become familiar with the fonts that you currently have available. Tens of thousands of licensed, commercial fonts are available to expand your collection. For the purposes of this book, you'll work with some common fonts; however, feel free to experiment with additional fonts at your leisure.

Type Family Dynamics

Fonts come in many varieties; each has a different look, feel, and flavor. Fonts are organized into type families that include a number of *weights* (thickness) and *styles* such as plain, italic, bold, and bold italic.

Broad type families use many different fonts, and small type families only include a few basic variations. Noncommercial fonts are often created for a specific title or purpose and may be inexpensive but often come in nonstandard sizes, which are limited in their variations.

Comparing Type Families

To compare type families, you can use any professional editing or design software that includes a text generator. This example uses Apple's Final Cut Pro application. Feel free to follow along using your own editing or design software.

Open a new project and create a new text object using the typed word *TEXT*.

NOTE: If you're not sure how to create a new piece of text within your application, take a moment to read over the software documentation to learn how to create text, and then proceed with the exercise.

After you've created a text object, you can change the font and style of the text.

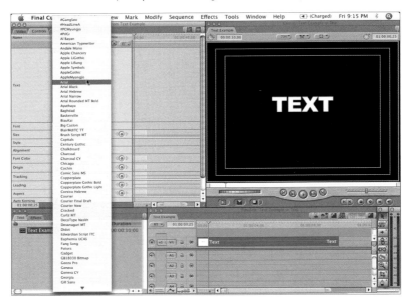

For this example, I'll change the text to the Arial font family. Within the Arial font family are several typeface varieties including Arial Black, Arial Hebrew, Arial Narrow, and Arial Rounded MT Bold.

There's an obvious family resemblance among the different Arial choices. They generally vary in thickness and have slight changes in appearance. The names are usually self-explanatory such as narrow or rounded.

NOTE: Your choices of fonts and styles may vary depending on the computer platform and fonts installed on your system.

Explore the different styles or typeface options ranging from Regular (Plain), Bold to Italic (oblique), or Bold Italic.

Arial Regular
Arial Italic
Arial Bold
Arial Bold Italic

The Arial font offers four typeface (style) varieties that represent the four primary text weights found in most commercial fonts. Now that you've seen an example of a typical font family, let's take a moment to explore a broad type family.

For this example, I'll change the text to the Helvetica type family, specifically Helvetica Neue.

Helvetica Neue - Condensed Bold
Helvetica Neue - Condensed Black
Helvetica Neue - UltraLight
Helvetica Neue - UltraLight Italic
Helvetica Neue - Light
Helvetica Neue - Light Italic
Helvetica Neue - Regular
Helvetica Neue - Italic
Helvetica Neue - Bold
Helvetica Neue - Bold Italic

The Helvetica Neue font has a broad type family, containing a wide range of weights that aren't commonly found in most type families.

If you'd like to compare some of the other font families and styles, choose a decorative font and test the different styles. Then explore some of the other font families available on your computer. Try to identify an example of an antique font, a symbol font, and serified and sans serif fonts. When you're finished exploring the different fonts available on your system, save and close your project.

Limit Your Fonts

Limit your project's titles to a total of three font families throughout. It's fine to vary the tonal weights such as bold or italic within the font families to broaden the emphasis, range, and depth of the titles. This is a basic graphic design rule that applies to everything from a movie poster to a business card and is equally effective in film and video titling. Limiting the number of different font families keeps the overall look cohesive, simple, clean, and effective. This doesn't mean that they all have to be boring or sans serif fonts. Choose three families that work well together or work well for the specific titling demands of your project. Mixing too many different font families within the same project or title looks cluttered and chaotic, and feels more like a ransom note than a professional title.

Three font families

Many font families

Adding Style to Text

Styling text includes selecting the type size, leading between lines of text, and alignment. You can further style text by adjusting the kerning, tracking, and horizontal and vertical scales.

Type size is measured by points (pt), which are 1/72 of an inch or about .351mm. Type sizes for film and video titles depend on the title category and final project format.

NOTE: Professional fonts come in standard sizes (6pt, 8pt, 9pt, 10pt, 11pt, 12pt, 13pt, 14pt, 18pt, 24pt, 36pt, 48pt, 64pt, 72pt, 96pt, 144pt, and 288pt).

Leading is the vertical space between lines of text and is named after the lead spacers used in old printing presses between the lines of type. Leading is usually the same size as the font. However, it can also be larger than the font size to create more space between lines or less than the font size to reduce the space between lines. Leading is sometimes called line spacing in editing and motion graphics applications.

This text is 48pt with Line Spacing set to 0. That means the leading is the same as the type size (48pt).

This text is 48pt with Line Spacing set to 2. That means the leading is 2pt more than the type size.

This text is 48pt with leading (line spacing) set less than the type size. As you can see, the ascending & descending characters are crashing.

Alignment refers to how the lines of text align to the right or left margins. The four primary alignment choices are left, right, center, and justified. You can apply these types of alignment to titles the same way you would a written document.

This text is aligned LEFT. Each line is flush with the left margin.

This text is aligned RIGHT. Each line is flush with the right margin.

This text is aligned CENTER. The center of each line is aligned while the left and right edges are not.

This text block is JUSTIFIED. That means space is added or removed between words so that both the left and right edges are flush to the left and right margins.

Tracking adjusts the horizontal space between all characters in a line of type. Increasing the tracking increases the amount of space (air) between characters, whereas decreasing the tracking decreases space between characters. Tracking is used to fit words into tighter spaces or stretch words or lines to fit a larger space.

no tracking changes

t r a c k i n g   a d d e d

tracking removed

Kerning allows you to adjust the horizontal space between specific characters based on the location of the cursor.

In the following example, there is a space between the first letter of each word and the rest of the word. This makes the word seem disjointed and loses the scripted text feel that the font suggests. To achieve the scripted text feel of the font, the kerning was adjusted between the "K" and "e" in Kerning, and the "c" and "h" in changes.

Identifying kerning issues and fixing them becomes second nature the more you work with text. Can you spot any other kerning issues in the example on the left that were fixed in the example on the right?

Kerning changes   *Kerning changes*

Cursor positioned to adjust kerning

Horizontal or vertical scale changes distort text to give it a longer, leaner look or a shorter, squattier look. This technique is often used to modify a font to fit a theme, or feel. Changing the horizontal or vertical scale of text is most commonly used in main titles and interjections. You can also gradually change the scale to make the text grow or shrink within the same line of text. In the leftmost example that follows, all of the text uses the Arial Black font with horizontal and vertical scale changes to the word big, and vertical changes to the word tall. In the example on the right, the perspective (corners) of the second line of text was changed to make the words slope downward and go from larger to smaller within the line.

Defining Your Space and Layout

The last element to contemplate before creating your title designs is the composition of the titles within the frame. Composition refers to the layout of the text, shapes, or images, and the use of space. Where you place your titles can be creative or practical depending on the situation. If you're making your composition and layout decision based on creativity and design aesthetics, you need to consider several principles. The five main principles of composition are rhythm, symmetrical, asymmetrical, space, and thirds.

Rhythm composition creates a sense of movement or visual pattern where the different elements fit together, similar to a musical rhythm or tempo.

Symmetrical composition is a more classic effect where you balance or mirror elements in relation to one another. Symmetrical composition style is visually pleasing and is often used in conservative projects such as commercials for financial institutes, political shows, and news. Aligning objects in size order, in neat rows, or in exact corners, or matching sizes in a mirrored fashion are symmetrical design choices.

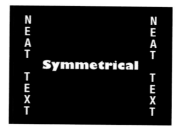

Asymmetrical composition is common in more modern and fun-looking projects such as a commercial for a hip new car or an extreme sports DVD. Asymmetrical composition is more free flowing, interesting, and eye stimulating. It doesn't mean haphazardly designed. Instead, the visual elements aren't aligned to any specific grid pattern or object and aren't necessarily lined up in neat rows, placed from smallest to largest, or organized in some logical manner.

 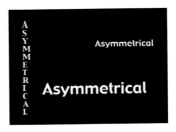

Space composition takes into consideration the empty or negative space as much as the space containing visual elements. Placing a title in a corner and leaving the remaining image text free is an example of space composition. Another example would be placing titles in the same space as other visual elements and intentionally leaving empty space in the frame.

Thirds composition is the most common composition principle and means the primary focus of the design is on one third of the frame while the remaining two thirds are empty or of secondary importance visually. Main titles appearing in the center third of the screen use this technique. Lower thirds and intellectual property rights text usually appear in the bottom third of the screen. Single title cards for credits generally appear in one third, whereas double title cards often appear at the same time in the upper and lower thirds.

 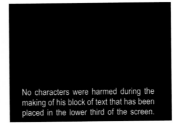

NOTE: All of the composition examples in the "Defining Your Space and Layout" section were created in empty frames without any competition from other motion pictures or graphic elements.

Working with Grids and Safe Zones

Grids, guides, and safe zones can be useful tools to align text within the frame or to make sure the text will be visible on any television or theatrical screen.

Professional motion graphics and design software such as After Effects, Photoshop, or Motion include rulers, grids, and guides for object alignment. Professional editing and motion graphics software includes safe zones for television and film zones for film projects. These zones are boundaries designed to show the part of the frame that will be visible within the television or film image regardless of the screen size, shape, and calibration. When you create titles, you see the entire frame size; however, the outer edges of the frame don't actually appear on most television sets or movie screens.

Video displayed on a computer monitor or large format digital screen will show the entire image. However, for those projects that will be seen on a television or projected in a theater, these boundaries are a necessary precaution. Think of safe zones as the mandatory margins that are required by printers for printing documents. Anything outside of the mandatory margin will not be printed or visible in the finished project.

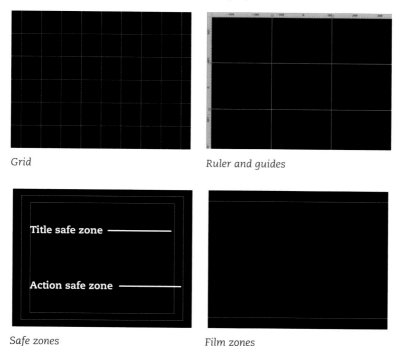

Grid

Ruler and guides

Safe zones

Film zones

TITLE TECHNIQUES AND VARIATIONS

BASIC SETUP FOR MAIN TITLES

Requirements

Software
  Any nonlinear editing or motion graphics software with title generator

Recommended Layout Features
  Title safe zones
  Ruler, grid, or guides turned on for text placement

Software Titling Advanced Features
  None

Time: 1–5 minutes

Preparation: Open a project and create a new text object.

Now that you understand the different categories of titles, criteria for choosing fonts, text styling options, and composition principles, you can start building basic titles.

You can apply the following basic titling techniques to a variety of projects. The titles in the examples are plain white text over a black background. However, don't let their simplicity fool you. They are also clean, classic, and highly effective.

You'll find full-resolution still images or QuickTime movies of each example on the companion DVD included with this book. The path is TITLE_DESIGN_ESSENTIALS > Chapter 1 > Main Titles.

Main Titles

The main title identifies a project's name and appears near the beginning of a show for television, training videos, and documentaries. Feature films usually include the main title as part of the opening title sequence. However, some filmmakers limit the opening title sequence and include the main title at the end.

Whenever you're designing titles, remember to trust your own instincts. It works or it doesn't; if you're on the fence and unsure, keep trying until you get it.

If you are torn between two options that work equally well, create titles using both options, and then let the client decide.

Main Title Checklist

Before you start creating your main titles, make sure you have a clear understanding of the overall project:

✔ What type of project is it? What is the emotional tone or genre? Choose a font family accordingly. For example, titles for an extreme sports video or western movie would look very different than the titles for a documentary about homeless children.

Selecting the right font family and style for your project's main title can be as challenging as it is rewarding when you find the right font. How do you know when you've found a font that works? Simple, you just know. Really.

✔ Is the title a sequel or part of a series? If so, the main titles should be similar if not identical in style to the first episode or film.

✔ Is the title long or short? The length of the title will affect your layout choices.

✔ Do contracts with talent require the title to be the same size as the names of the stars, director, or producer? If so, will they be single or double card credits, and how long will the names be? In this situation, it is sometimes easiest to create the opening credits first to determine size and placement. Then create a main title of equal size and placement as the credits as contracts dictate.

✔ On what size screen will the final project be primarily viewed? If it is a theatrical screen, the projected titles will be very large so they don't necessarily need to be full screen. If the project is streaming video or is intended to play on an iPod, phone, or other portable device, the image will be very small so the titles should be larger on the screen to compensate for the small image size.

001 – THE CLASSIC MAIN TITLE

The classic main title is the Old Faithful of titles. It's easy to create and works well for any type of project with a short title of one to three words. There are no frills here, but it's tasteful and effective.

DV NTSC 720x480
Helvetica Neue—bold, 48pt

DV NTSC 720x480
Helvetica Neue—bold, 36pt

Type your project's main title in capital letters. Move the text to the center of the screen, if it is not already centered. Choose a font that works for your project. If you are unsure of which font to use, try Geneva, Helvetica, Helvetica Neue, Gill Sans, or Arial fonts for a clean classic look. To add more personality to the title, try a decorative, antique, or script font to taste.

Once you have selected a font, change the font to a size that is easy to read, yet still well within the title safe zone.

If your title is more than one word, you can also separate the words on different lines in the center of the screen for a stacked look rather than a sentence look. For stacked text, try varying the size of the text on the different lines to emphasize certain words over others.

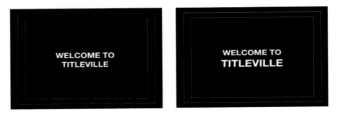

TIP: Always modify font sizes within the text parameter controls. If you change the scale of text by resizing the object or dragging the edges of the object, you'll be stretching the smaller size font to make it larger. This method will likely make the stretched text look unfocused and pixilated.

002 – THE CLASSIC WITH A TWIST

You can add a creative twist to the classic main title by modifying the style of the text for some or all of the words.

Simply prepare the text as in the preceding example except vary the weight of some or all of the text among bold, normal, or narrow, and sprinkle with italicized text to taste.

NOTE: Use all caps or uppercase and lowercase? Generally, the main title of a project is written in all capital letters. However, for long titles or a more casual feeling title, some filmmakers use uppercase and lowercase letters.

003 – SOLO IN THE CORNER POCKET

Single word titles are a challenge because there are so many layout and style choices it's difficult to decide what is best for the project.

Shake things up and take advantage of the space onscreen by placing the title in one of the corners rather than in the center. Avoiding the center of the screen adds an element of surprise to the title for maximum impact.

Create your title, and then align it near one of the title safe boundaries. Choose your font carefully based on the mood and feel of the project. If you're using a standard serif or sans serif font, try modifying the text style.

004 – DIAMOND SOLO

The diamond solo, a variation on the solo text, places a single word title near the title safe boundary but away from the corners or center of the screen. As with the other solo text, varying the style and font will greatly affect the overall look and feel of the text.

Long Main Titles

Working with a long title can be challenging because of the length of text that needs to be tastefully displayed. In this case, size does matter, as well as the readability of the font.

Create a text object with the project's full title. Choose a title layout that suits the project and screen size. (See the sidebar "Font Size vs. Screen Size and Viewer's Perspective" later in this chapter.) The size of the font should be determined based on the screen size and relative distance of the audience from the screen.

005 – THE CLASSIC LONG TITLE

The classic main title technique is the same for long titles as it is for short titles. The difference is the length of the text.

Single line of text   *Stacked and centered text*

NOTE: Long titles are usually created using capital letters; however, uppercase and lowercase letters can be used to make the title feel more like a sentence or a statement, or purely to set a different tone to the title.

006 – THE PYRAMID

An interesting way to display a long main title is to center the text and break it into lines of progressively larger point sizes. This technique works well for humorous projects, news special features, and project titles that benefit from emphasis on the last (largest) line of text.

Stacked, centered, and size varied

007 – DOUBLE–DECKER IN THE CORNER POCKET

Separating a title into two lines with varied font sizes or styles and justifying it to an adjacent corner is ideal for long titles to emphasize the beginning or end of the title.

Left justified, varied size, and style

008 – CORNER POCKET STACKED OR SINGLE

The classic title design is very predictable and expected. Varying the main title's placement to a corner, whether stacked or as a single line, makes a title more interesting. This technique will likely catch the viewer's attention because it is unpredictable and will also suggest that the project is different, unique, and possibly unpredictable as well.

Stacked, left justified   Single line, italicized

NOTE: All of the long main title examples would work well for a television or movie screen. Some of the examples would be difficult to read on a small portable media device because of the relative size of the screen.

Nonfiction Series Main Titles

Nonfiction series main titles are for multipart documentaries, news specials, or training video series. Television episodic series use more complex animated titles.

The challenge of nonfiction series titles is not only their length, but also differentiating the title of the series and the title of the episode. You also need to decide if you want to add a colon or a dash between the series title and the episode title.

Keep in mind, if all of the text is the same size and style, and is grouped together, it feels like one long title instead of a series title.

This example reads like a long main title rather than a nonfiction series title.

Font Size vs. Screen Size and Viewer's Perspective

How do you know what size font to use for your titles? Font sizes are often determined by the perspective size of text, not necessarily the actual size of the screen. In fact, the perceived size of the text is directly related to the distance and size of the screen.

Consider three elements when choosing a font size for a title:

- The frame size of the project that you will be titling
- The screen size where the project will be viewed
- The audience's perspective (viewing distance) from the screen

You choose a font size relative to a project's frame size. For example, 24pt is relatively large on a multimedia project with a frame size of 160 x 120. The same 24pt text appears smaller on a multimedia project with a frame size of 320 x 240.

24pt text, 160 x 120 frame

24pt text, 320 x 240 frame

And 24pt text in a DV NTSC video project with a frame size of 720 x 480 appears to be much smaller because the frame size is bigger. In all three cases the 24pt text remains the exact same size, only the frame dimensions change.

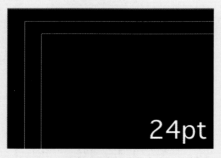

24pt text, 720 x 480 (partial) frame

You also need to consider the size of the screen where the project will be viewed. If a DV NTSC project is shrunk down to fit a 320 x 240 video iPod screen, the text will shrink as well.

But what if the project will be viewed at different frame sizes? In that case, create the titles at the largest frame size.

Finally, think about the viewing distance between the audience and the screen.

A small portable multimedia device, such as a video iPod, has a screen that is only a few inches across. A person viewing media on the device may hold it close or at arm's length, but either way it will still display a small image.

An average television set is around 30 inches across, and the perceived size will be relatively the same from anywhere in the room.

A movie screen in a theater could be over 30 feet across and appears much larger to those in the front row than those in the back of the theater. Regardless of the position in the theater, the screen will always appear large. Text on a movie screen may appear 10 feet wide, and the same text on a television screen will only appear 10 inches wide.

Example of Titles and Viewing Distance

Video billboards, such as the ones you see in Times Square or in Las Vegas, may be over 50 feet tall, but the average audience could be located anywhere from across the street or several blocks away; therefore, the perceived size varies depending on the viewers' position. From a block or two away, a video billboard's perceived size is a few inches, similar to that of a portable media device.

NOTE: If your software, such as Apple's Motion, allows you to modify selected text separately, you can create your full-series title in one text object. If you are using software that makes all text within an object the same, such as Apple's Final Cut Pro, you'll need to create two or three separate text objects to build your series main title.

Large or bold text generally feels more stressed or emphasized, whereas small or italicized text is more subtle and seems less important.

Emphasis on series title   *Emphasis on episode title*

Use of colon before part number   *Use of dash before episode number*

Experiment with different text alignments, styles, and layouts.

009 – MIXED–BAG CORNER ALIGNMENT

The mixed-bag corner alignment title technique uses variations in the font family, style, and use of uppercase or lowercase letters to differentiate between the title elements.

Start with the series title and part on one line, and the episode title beneath. Align the two lines to either an upper or lower corner. Finally, vary the type style or family for each element. In this example, the title was aligned to the upper-right corner. The series title was created in all caps and italic, the series part in uppercase and lowercase italic, and the episode title in bold italics and all caps. Separate the series title, part, and episode using three different type styles.

010 – MIXED–BAG CENTER ALIGNMENT

Follow the steps for the mixed-bag corner alignment text (009), only change the alignment to center. Choose between the upper, middle, or lower third of the frame for center text placement.

011 – MIXED–BAG WITH SPLIT PERSONALITY

Create a mixed-bag title, and then add space between the series title and the episode title. This technique is ideal for introducing a different font family to the series title or the episode title to add personality. Try fun or interesting fonts to add flavor to the title.

In the example on the left, the series title has a fun font to give the impression that the series is also fun. The example on the right uses interesting and unique fonts with personality for both the series title and the episode title to make it seem like the overall project will be interesting and less institutional.

Small Format Main Titles

Podcasts, streaming videos, Web clips, and projects created for handheld media devices are generally watched on very small screens or frame sizes, so the titles need to be designed accordingly.

TIP: For small format main titles:

- Use bold fonts that are easy to read on a small screen.

- Preview the titles at the actual size they will be screened, such as 320 x 240, to see if they are clearly legible.

- Stay away from thin font styles, especially ultra thin fonts with italics because they are very difficult to read on a small screen.

CREDITS TECHNIQUES AND VARIATIONS

Credits that appear at the beginning of a project in the opening title sequence are usually single or double title cards for the key actors and crew. Credits that appear in the closing title sequence are often a combination of single cards and scrolling text that includes the entire cast, crew, and support personnel. Title cards get their name from the early titles and credits that were created on actual cards, and then filmed one at a time and edited into a silent movie.

You'll find full-resolution still images or QuickTime movies of each credit example on the companion DVD included with this book. The path is TITLE_DESIGN_ESSENTIALS > Chapter 1 > Credits.

Credits Checklist

Before you start creating your credits, here are a few considerations you should think about.

✔ Do you have a complete list of names for credits? If not, make sure that you get the complete list and add the remaining names before the project is finished.

✔ Are the names spelled correctly? It's best to get a list of names from either the legal department or producer's team because they will most likely spell the names correctly. If there is any doubt, make a note to double-check the spelling of all names. If you don't, you'll find out they are incorrect the hard way during an early screening when the cast and crew are most likely to see the project for the first time.

✔ Are there contractual requirements for the credits? If so, become familiar with the rules and create the credits accordingly. If a contract dictates that certain credits be the same size and treatment as the main title, you may want to create the main title first as a template. Otherwise, you can create the credits first, and then create a main title to match.

Single Title Card

Single title cards are also referred to as a single credit, solo credit, or just credit. They can include a name plus a job title or just a name. In recent years credits have also become a legal issue that is specifically stated in a production contract. For example, stars and key

---

> **BASIC SETUP FOR CREDITS**
>
> **Requirements**
>
> *Software*
>   Any nonlinear editing or motion graphics software with title generator
>
> *Recommended Layout Features*
>   Title safe zones
>   Ruler, grid, or guides turned on for text placement
>
> *Software Titling Advanced Features*
>   None
>
> **Time:** 1–5 minutes
>
> **Preparation:** Open a project and create a new text object. Create two text objects for double title cards if the layout involves different areas of the frame.

positions like director and producer contractually must get solo credits that are the same size and style as the main title.

The various Hollywood unions, such as Screen Actors Guild (SAG), Directors Guild of America (DGA), and Writers Guild of America (WGA) have union guidelines and rules for credits that appear onscreen.

NOTE: Most of the examples in this chapter focus on the credit text, not on the position in the frame. The text may all look centered and scaled; however, the text could actually be placed anywhere in the frame.

012 – CLASSIC SOLO CREDIT

Like classic titles, the classic solo credit aligns the text to the center of the screen. The classic solo credit uses the same font, family, style, and case for both the name and the job title.

Close view of credit   Full-frame view

013 – MIXED–BAG SOLO CREDIT

The mixed-bag credits vary the case, style, font, or size between the job title and the name. There are endless combinations that work effectively. Choose one that fits well with the look and feel of your project, and use the same combination for all of the single title cards.

014 – MIXED NAME CREDIT

The mixed name credit technique is a more contemporary treatment of names in both single and double title cards, and uses a different style, font, case, or size between the first and last names. When creating mixed name credits, the space between the first and last names is optional depending on the overall look you are trying to achieve. This type of credit text is often found in films and television shows that are quirky, comedic, or stylish and unique—just like the titles.

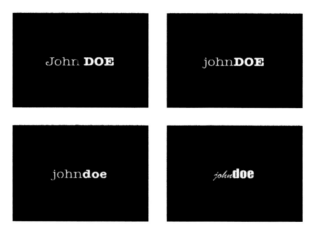

TIP: When creating single title cards, start with the longest name and use that as a basis for selecting the font size, style, and text layout. Once the first single title card is finished, you can use that as a template for making the rest of the single credits.

Double Title Card

Double title card credits involve two names onscreen at the same time. Why the same time instead of one after the other? When a movie features two movie stars who are in equal starring roles, their contracts may demand equal billing. Showing the names at the same time onscreen suggests they are equally important. If the names were shown one at a time, there might be some speculation as to which star is more important. Double title cards are also used for supporting roles that warrant mention in the opening title sequence. Since they are supporting roles, two, three, and even four names may be listed at once.

Credits Techniques and Variations

015 – OPPOSITE PAIRS

Placing the names in opposite positions on the screen gives them the necessary sense of equality without crowding them together in the frame. The varying positions include corners, upper and lower centers, left and right sides, or slightly offset from center.

016 – SUPPORTING STACK

Stack and center the supporting cast names alphabetically unless otherwise required by contract. For variety you can also left or right justify the names.

017 – CORNER POCKET PAIRS

Corner pocket pairs is another option for supporting cast names. Place a pair of names stacked in any corner and then align the text left or right to match the corner. Although this technique is most commonly used for two names, it can also work for three or four names if needed.

Shared Credit

Shared credits are used when more than one person is credited for the same work, such as writing, editing, or directing. The names are usually listed in order of importance (amount of contribution) from top to bottom, or if the contribution is equal, they are listed alphabetically.

018 – CLASSIC SHARED WITH MIXED SIZE

Since all classic text is the same, centered on the screen, here is a shared credit version that varies the font size between the job title and the names to make it a little more interesting. This technique, which uses all caps, is very common in both feature films and television show titles.

019 – MIXED SHARED RIGHT OR LEFT

The mixed shared credit variation is great for aligning the text to the left or right side, or corners of the frame.

Once again the mixed styles, fonts, sizes, or cases help separate the job title from the name while still giving the names emphasis. This version is also useful if you are aligning the text to an object within the image on the screen. It's fine to add variety between the job title and the "and" between names. Just be sure to style the names the same way.

NOTE: Scrolling credits that appear at the end of a project involve animation and are included in Chapter 4, "Working with Basic Animation."

Sample Contract Paragraph Re: Credits
(Single, Double, and Shared)

Sample of a possible screenwriter's contract:

The writer's credit should appear in the main credits of the film, on a single card, in a size and type equal to the size and type of any other writer's credit. The credit should also appear in all screen and paid ads if the director, producer, and any other writer receives credit. If the writer is not the only writer, then the writer will have to share the writing credit.

Sample of a possible composer's contract:

The composer will expect to receive credit in three media: the picture, paid advertisements, and the soundtrack album. Credit will appear in the form "Music By..." The credit should appear on a separate card with size and type equal to the producer, writer, and director credits. The composer will expect to have his credit appear whenever the producer, writer, or director credit appears.

TEXT BLOCK TECHNIQUES

Text blocks come in two varieties. One contains blocks of text intended to be read and comprehended, such as a quote from a movie critic, a short legal disclaimer, or a text prologue before a movie. The other contains text blocks that are likely not to be read and comprehended. These are the *fine-print* paragraphs used in commercials for products such as car loans or pharmaceuticals that are too small to read on an average television and are not onscreen long enough to read unless you are a world-class speed reader. These blocks of text are included to fulfill a legal obligation, like the blocks of fine-print text that you might find in a printed contract or product pamphlet.

You'll find full-resolution still images or QuickTime movies of each text block example on the companion DVD included with this book. The path is TITLE_DESIGN_ESSENTIALS > Chapter 1 > Text Blocks.

Text Block Checklist

Before you start creating text blocks, here are a few considerations you should think about.

✔ Do you have a hard copy of the text, or does it exist electronically in a word processing document? It's best not to write the text on the fly for a large block; you're more likely to make mistakes. If it is on hard copy, you'll have to retype it. If it is in a word processor, you can usually copy and paste it into your graphics program.

✔ Has the content of the text been edited, spell checked, and grammatically corrected? Glaring errors are unprofessional. If you can't check it yourself, find someone who can.

✔ Is the text block a legal disclaimer? If so, it probably won't be onscreen long enough to actually be read, but just in case, make sure the text comes from a lawyer, legal aide, or the legal department, and that a lawyer signs off on it.

BASIC SETUP FOR TEXT BLOCKS

Requirements
Software
   Any nonlinear editing or motion graphics software with title generator

Recommended Layout Features
   Title safe zones

   Justification (full or partial)

   Leading or line spacing controls

Software Titling Advanced Features
   Spell check

Time: 5–25 minutes depending on the length of the text block and your typing speed

Preparation: Open a project and create a new text object. If the text is available in a word processing document, copy and paste the text into the text object. Otherwise, type the entire block before attempting layout.

Short Text Blocks and Paragraphs

Short text blocks include prologues, epilogues, short blurbs, and quotes. They may be placed anywhere in the frame and can be aligned left, right, center, or justified depending on the layout. Since short text blocks are generally intended to be read and comprehended, it's a good idea to choose a simple, easy-to-read serifed or sans serifed font. Also, make sure that the font size is appropriate for legibility and placement in the frame. Generally, the font size should be as large as needed for clarity, but not so large that it dominates the screen.

Setting Line Spacing

Setting the line spacing or leading equal to the type size is referred to as *set solid* and makes text easy to read for short paragraphs or individual words on separate lines. For easier readability of large blocks of text, it is common to add 2pts of leading to the actual type size. For example, if you create three lines of 18pt text, you would use a leading of 20pt, or line spacing of 2. On the other hand, if the leading is set lower than the type size, the strokes that ascend above or descend below the base lines of text may overlap (crash). Crashing lines of text together may look stylish for certain projects and fonts, but may look like a distracting text mistake in other situations. You can tighten or loosen the leading as needed to fit the text into a smaller or larger space to achieve an overall look.

020 – CLASSIC SHORT BLOCK

The classic short block variation is aligned center but not necessarily placed in the center of the frame. There is room for flexibility in the font style; however, the font family should be clean and easy to read.

021 – RIGHT ALIGNED SHORT BLOCK

Set the text alignment to right for this clean-looking short block. This variation works well for quotes. Like the classic short block, the text style is flexible. Feel free to mix the style between the quote and the tag line.

> *"Amazing!... It was the best*
> *text block I've ever read.*
> *I'd read it again and again."*
>
> -- Ms. Reader

022 – JUSTIFIED SHORT BLOCK

Although the justified short block variation is most commonly used for large text blocks, it also works for short blocks containing several sentences. This technique is most common for blurbs, epilogues, and prologues. When justifying a short block, you'll need to manually break up the text into separate lines by pressing Return. Be careful not to leave too much air (space) between words.

> "Predictable and uneventful....
> Such square and evenly spaced
> text in a block was expected.
> The effort was fully justified."

Large Text Blocks

The secret to creating effective text blocks is the justification. Although you can align them right, center, or left, justifying the text will make it look, feel, and read more like a block of printed text.

Some editing and design software applications have additional justification parameters such as partial justification and full justification. Partial justification works with either left, right, or center justification and leaves a bit of a fringed edge but doesn't add as much air between words. Full justification will add as much air (space) as needed to force a line to start on the left margin and end on the right margin. Full justification looks more like printed text and looks professional.

Text Block Techniques

TIP: Film and video editors aren't necessarily text editors, and vice versa. If you are typing a large text block in your graphics program, you may want to copy and paste the text in a word processor to perform a spell check and grammar check, and then make the necessary changes. You could also start by typing in a word processor, and then copying and pasting the polished text into your graphics project.

023 – LOWER HALF BLOCK

Most all text blocks are placed in the lower half of the frame. Usually, text blocks are very small and stashed in the lower half as a legal obligation. Keep the font clean and simple. The justification makes all the difference in the look and feel of the block. Almost all text blocks are fully justified for an official, professional look.

NOTE: Make sure the text is within the title safe boundary so it will be fully visible on any television screen.

Center justified

Full justification (left and right)

This block of text may be included in a car commercial to explain all of the risks and terms of the loan agreements. It also tells that to get the advertised discount it must be a Thursday with a full moon and the average temperature above 70 degrees. Also, the discount only applies if you live in the state of confusion and have never owned a car. This offer is not valid with any other offer, or for any person with an education level above primary school. All requests for this discount must be submitted in writing within 1 hour of reading this disclaimer. Failure to submit request in writing within the time specified forfeits any claims for discount now or in the future.

Partial justified, left

This block of text may be included in a car commercial to explain all of the risks and terms of the loan agreements. It also tells that to get the advertised discount it must be a Thursday with a full moon and the average temperature above 70 degrees. Also, the discount only applies if you live in the state of confusion and have never owned a car. This offer is not valid with any other offer, or for any person with an education level above primary school. All requests for this discount must be submitted in writing within 1 hour of reading this disclaimer. Failure to submit request in writing within the time specified forfeits any claims for discount now or in the future.

Partial justified, center

Avoid Rivers in Your Text Blocks

If spaces between letters are stacked up from line to line in justified text, they create a visual "river" of space that seems to travel up the height of a text block. You can easily dam up a river by changing the line breaks to redistribute words and move the spaces so they don't line up so precisely.

This block of text may be included in a car commercial to explain all of the risks and terms of the loan agreements. It also tells that to get the advertised discount it must be a Thursday with a full moon and the average temperature above 70 degrees. Also, the discount only applies if you live in the state of confusion and have never owned a car. This offer is not valid with any other offer, or for any person with an education level above primary school. All requests for this discount must be submitted in writing within 1 hour of reading this disclaimer. Failure to submit request in writing within the time specified forfeits any claims for discount now or in the future.

Justified text block with multiple rivers running vertically up through the text block.

This block of text may be included in a car commercial to explain all of the risks and terms of the loan agreements. It also tells that to get the advertised discount it must be a Thursday with a full moon and the average temperature above 70 degrees. Also, the discount only applies if you live in the state of confusion and have never owned a car. This offer is not valid with any other offer, or for any person with   an education level aboveprimary school. All requests for this discount must be submitted in writing within 1 hour of reading this disclaimer. Failure to submit request in writing within the time specified forfeits any claims for discount now or in the future.

Justified text is redistributed between lines to diminish the rivers.

Text Block Techniques

KEY INFORMATION TEXT TECHNIQUES

BASIC SETUP FOR KEY INFORMATION TEXT

Requirements
Software
  Any nonlinear editing or motion graphics software with title generator

Recommended Layout Features
  Title safe zones

  Ruler, grid, or guides turned on for text placement

Software Titling Advanced Features
  None

Time: 1–5 minutes

Preparation: Open a project and create a new text object. Create separate objects for each piece of information if they will be placed in different areas of the frame.

Key information text is most commonly found in commercials, training videos, Web sites, and DVD or CD-ROM catalog-type projects. Key information text should be prominent, clear, and easy to read. This text is often the most important of the entire piece, especially if the desired result of a project is for a viewer to respond to the information by dialing a phone, attending an event, or visiting a company or Web site.

Generally, such information is extremely important and is the purpose of the entire project. In that case, it doesn't have to be fancy or animated, it just has to be clear, legible, and onscreen long enough for viewers to read and remember.

TIP: Fancy, frilly, abstract fonts may be fine for a poster, company logo, or possibly the main title of a project without a strict time constraint, but aren't recommended for video titles that are only visible for a finite amount of time and need to be read and processed quickly. Use easy to read and recognize fonts for key information text so the viewer will comprehend the information in a short amount of time.

Creating a phone number and date may not seem like much of a challenge, but actually there is a lot of responsibility that comes with key information text.

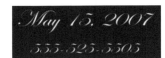

Notice the two examples of key information text. In the example on the left, a simple sans serif font was used; in the example on the right, a more decorative and exciting font was used. Which would be more effective if it was only onscreen for six seconds?

You'll find full-resolution still images or QuickTime movies of each key information example on the companion DVD included with this book. The path is TITLE_DESIGN_ESSENTIALS > Chapter 1 > Key Information.

Key Information Text Checklist

Before you start creating your key information text, here are a few considerations you should think about.

✔ Are the dates that you have accurate? If not, make sure that you get the final dates before the project is finished. This is especially important for projects that revolve around dates that are tentative or contingent on weather.

✔ Is the address, phone number, or Web site information correct? Double-check everything with more than one source if possible. Why? Because no matter what you are told by the producer, director, or an assistant, if there is a mistake, the one who created the text will always be blamed.

✔ Is the text easy to read and comprehend?

024 – CLASSIC KEY WITH MIXED SIZE

Classic centered text is common for titles and credits. Key information text, on the other hand, is usually displayed over other images so it only dominates the screen if there are no other priority images. Classic key text is usually reserved for showing key information at the end of a project, such as a commercial or public service announcement. Mixed sizes are handy for emphasizing elements like phone numbers and fitting long text like Web addresses.

The example on the left has very large text that is aligned to the center of the frame and was designed for a small format project. The example on the right is a normal size for a television screen and has the phone number in the center of the frame for emphasis, followed by the additional key information.

025 – LOWER SET SINGLE OR DOUBLE KEY

Traditionally, a single or double line of key information text is placed at the bottom of the screen to leave room for other visuals. The size, font, and style should be determined by legibility and limitations of space. Of course this information can also be placed in the middle or upper third of the frame if needed.

026 – BUSINESS CARD LAYOUT

If you have the luxury of using the entire frame for your key information text, with no competing images, you can design the layout as you would a business card. Try either symmetrical or asymmetrical layouts to distribute the information on the frame. Just remember, like a business card, keep it simple and make sure the text is easy to read.

Intellectual Property Rights and Short Disclaimer Techniques

Projects often require simple intellectual property rights such as trademarks, copyrights or patents, and short disclaimers. These text elements are almost always located at the bottom of the frame and use a font that matches the credits or main title.

Copyright text is usually at the very end of a film, video, or television show. Additional intellectual property rights text is used as needed in commercials, music videos, and sales and training videos.

Intellectual Property Rights Checklist

Before you start creating your intellectual property rights or short disclaimers text, here are a few considerations you should think about.

✔ If you are creating copyright text, does it require Roman numerals or standard numbers? If you are rusty with your Roman numerals see the Conversion Table in Appendix A at the back of the book.

✔ If you are adding trademark, patent, or copyright information, clear it with a legal department if possible for accuracy.

✔ Short disclaimers are very common and are nearly invisible. If you are working on a commercial or training video that includes a product that may affect people's health in any way, you'll need a disclaimer. Check with the legal department or client for wording.

You'll find full-resolution still images or QuickTime movies of each intellectual property rights example on the companion DVD included with this book. The path is TITLE_DESIGN_ESSENTIALS > Chapter 1 > Intellectual Property Rights.

027 – CLASSIC RIGHTS

Classic intellectual property text is always center justified and located within the title safe zone at the bottom of the frame. Use a clean serifed or sans serifed font, or a font that matches the other text on the frame, such as the credits.

BASIC SETUP FOR INTELLECTUAL PROPERTY RIGHTS AND SHORT DISCLAIMERS TEXT

Requirements
Software
Any nonlinear editing or motion graphics software with title generator

Recommended Layout Features
Title safe zones

Ruler, grid, or guides turned on for text placement

Software Titling Advanced Features
None

Time: 1–5 minutes

Preparation: Open a project and create a new text object.

NOTE: Turn to Appendix A at the back of the book for keyboard shortcuts to create trademark, copyright, and patent symbols.

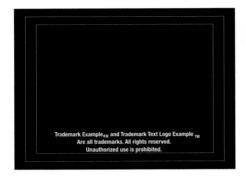

028 – CLASSIC RIGHTS IN CAPS

A slight variation to the classic rights technique is to use the Capitals font or all uppercase letters to add a more serious legal feel to the text.

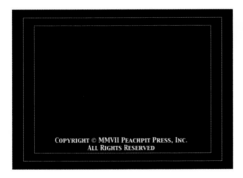

029 – CLASSIC SHORT DISCLAIMER

The classic short disclaimer is located in the lower center of the frame, similar to the classic intellectual property rights. These short statements are most commonly seen in commercials. Disclaimers include statements like, "Prescription only," "Results vary," and "Simulation."

Check with your doctor before starting any new exercise program.

CHAPTER 2

Spicing Up Text with Drop Shadows, Outlines, and Glows

Now that you understand the basics of creating titles, you can spice them up with shadows, outlines, and glows. These features are designed to be practical or fun depending on the situation. They can be practical for adding definition to text, separating it from the background, or adding emphasis. They can also be fun to accessorize text to add more personality and steal attention from other text or elements within the frame.

Drop Shadow
Outline Glow

NOTE: These variations are designed to work with any professional editing or motion graphics application. The examples in this chapter were all created in Apple's Motion application unless otherwise indicated.

Understanding Drop Shadows

A drop shadow's primary function is to separate text from the background by simulating a shadow. This is usually a black shadow below white text on a background that is anything but black. You can also apply drop shadows to text to make the text more interesting.

Drop shadows are usually dark colors and are generally used over light- or medium-colored backgrounds. When using a drop shadow over a dark background, the shadow color needs to be much lighter than the background to show up.

The controls for modifying drop shadows vary slightly from application to application. However, they always include the six main controls: scale, color, opacity, blur, distance, and angle.

Scale

The drop shadow scale is measured in relation to the size of the text. A scale of 100% means the shadow is the same size as the text. Most drop shadow techniques use the shadow at 100% scale.

NOTE: Assume that the scale for the drop shadows in the following variations is 100% unless otherwise noted.

Color

You can read more about using color in the next chapter. For now it is just important to know that the drop shadow color needs to be different from the background and the text. Using an opposite or contrasting color is a good way to go; so if the text is white, use a black drop shadow and vice versa.

Opposite text and shadow color

Opacity, Blur, and Distance

A drop shadow's opacity, blur, and distance (also called offset) are used in combination to create the illusion of space between the text and the background. Opacity is how solid the shadow appears. Blur refers to the focus of the shadow, and distance represents how far the shadow is from the text. If there is no blur, the focus of the shadow is sharp and crisp. Adding blur defocuses the shadow, making it appear blurry.

Think of drop shadows as real shadows. The farther an object is from the background, the greater the distance of the shadow. The closer an object is to the background, the shorter the distance of the shadow. Once you have established the distance, you can adjust the blur and opacity of the shadow accordingly.

Angle

The angle controls vary slightly between applications; however, their function is always the same. The angle control either adjusts the angle of the light source or the angle at which the shadow appears from behind the text. Experiment with your application to see how the angle controls affect the shadow, and then adjust as needed to achieve the desired look.

NOTE: Professional editing and graphics software that includes a title generator should also have a drop shadow feature. If you've never worked with the drop shadow features in your software, take a moment to familiarize yourself with the drop shadow controls.

DROP SHADOW TECHNIQUES AND VARIATIONS

**DROP SHADOW SETUP
(APPLY TO PREPARED
BASIC TITLES)**

Requirements
Software
    Any nonlinear editing or
    motion graphics software
    with title generator

Recommended Layout Features
    None

*Software Titling Advanced
Features*
    Drop shadow feature
    with controls: blur,
    scale, distance or offset,
    opacity, color
    Angle control (optional)

Time: 1–5 minutes

Preparation: Open a project
containing a basic title.
Select the text object and
turn on or apply the drop
shadow feature.

Once you understand the function of drop shadows, you can start applying them to your titles. You can use drop shadows with all types of titles.

These variations show plain white or black text; however, you could substitute the black with any dark color and substitute the white with any light or pastel color. You'll find details about working with color in Chapter 3, "Enhancing Text with Color and Gradients."

You'll find full-resolution still images or QuickTime movies of each example on the companion DVD included with this book. The path is TITLE_DESIGN_ESSENTIALS > Chapter 2 > Drop Shadow.

Drop Shadow Checklist

Before you add a drop shadow to your text, make sure you have a clear understanding as to why you are adding the shadow.

✔   Do you want to add dimension to the project by separating the text from the background?

✔   If you're adding a shadow to show distance between the text and the background, how far do you want them to be separated?

✔   Is there a visible light source that you'd like to cause the shadow? If so, you'll need to adjust the shadow angle accordingly.

✔   Does the text seem dull, lifeless, and need a little spicing up?

✔   Do you want to emphasize certain words and phrases with the use of a shadow?

✔   Do you want the small print to be easier to read?

TIP: If you are working with an application that does not have a drop shadow feature, you can create a similar effect by duplicating the text object. Place the duplicate below the original text. Change the color of the duplicate to the shadow color. Then offset, resize, and blur the duplicate as needed to create the desired look.

030 – THE CLASSIC SHADOW (AKA THE DEFAULT)

The classic shadow is the most common drop shadow look and adds a distinctive shadow to the text. This style of drop shadow is often the default setting for most applications when the feature is enabled, applied, or turned on.

The classic shadow shows depth without too much distance between the text and the background. You can create a classic shadow by setting the drop shadow parameters to Distance 3–5, Blur 0, Opacity 75%, and Angle 315 degrees.

NOTE: Parameter settings may vary depending on your application. Experiment with your settings to match the look in the examples.

If your application does not include angle controls, chances are they are already set so that the shadow points toward the lower right of the text.

Distance or Offset 5

Distance or Offset 3

031 – THE FLUFFY CLASSIC SHADOW

The fluffy classic shadow is created by raising the opacity of the shadow while simultaneously adding a little blur to give it a soft fluffy look. The trick to the fluffy classic shadow is to add just enough blur to give it a soft look without losing the definition of the shadow. This technique looks great on main titles, interjections, and credits. It is not recommended for block text.

To create the fluffy classic shadow, modify the settings as follows: Distance 3–5, Blur 2–3, Opacity 100%, and Angle 315 degrees.

Distance 3, Blur 3

Distance 5, Blur 2

032 – THE CLOUD SHADOW

The cloud shadow is named after the soft cloud of drop shadow beneath the text. Unlike the fluffy classic shadow where the shadow is soft but still resembles the text, the cloud shadow is blurred so much that the cloud-like shadow merely resembles the shape of the overall text. One of the tricks to creating the cloud shadow is the use of scale. By making the scale of the drop shadow much larger than the text (at least 150%), it creates a larger cloud behind the text. If the scale is the same as the text, it looks more like a smudge than a cloud.

The cloud shadow is useful for making text easier to see on a busy moving background.

To create the cloud shadow, start with the fluffy classic settings and then modify them to Distance 0, Blur 20–30, Opacity 100%, and Scale 150%.

033 – THE ECHO SHADOW

The echo shadow defies the laws of physics in that the shadow doesn't become more blurred or lose opacity at a distance. Instead of using the shadow to add dimension, the echo technique uses the shadow more to repeat the text (like an echo). This technique doubles the emphasis on a word because it literally doubles the word. The echo is most commonly used with interjection text for words like BUY NOW, FREE, and SUPER SALE. It is not recommended for block text, rights, crawling text, or lower thirds.

To create the echo shadow, start with the classic settings, and then adjust the distance or offset to move the shadow away from the actual text.

The echo shadow settings are Distance 30–100, Blur 0, Opacity 75%, and Angle 315 degrees.

Distance 33

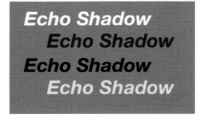

Distance 60

034 – THE FORESHADOW

As the name suggests, the foreshadow technique places the shadow before the text. The secret to making the foreshadow work is to make sure that the shadow angle is even with the text (angle 180), and then change the distance so that the shadow comes first, followed closely by the text.

This type of shadow alignment works well for main titles, credits, interjections, and lower thirds. As with most stylish shadows, it's not recommended for text blocks.

Start by changing the angle to make the shadow even with the text. Next, change the distance or offset until the shadow is before the text. Feel free to experiment with the distance to move the shadow closer or farther from the text.

The foreshadow settings are Opacity 75%, Angle 180, and Distance 5.

035 – THE AFTSHADOW

The aftshadow variation is the opposite of the foreshadow. Instead of coming before the text, the aftshadow comes after. This shadow also works well with main titles, interjections, credits, and lower thirds.

Start by making the angle of the shadow the same as the text (Angle 0 in most applications.) Then modify the distance or offset to slowly move the shadow toward the right until it appears after the text.

The aftshadow settings are Opacity 75%, Angle 0, and Distance 5.

036 – THE LOOMING SHADOW

The looming shadow is a rare but effective drop shadow that usually appears in main titles or credits for comedies, mysteries, or horror films. This quirky looking shadow gets its name from the fact that it seems to be looming over the text. As with most shadow effects, the looming shadow is simple to accomplish.

Start by setting the Angle to 0 and the Scale to 200%. Then modify the opacity of the shadow as desired. Feel free to modify the scale as needed for a larger or smaller looming effect.

The looming shadow settings are Distance 0, Opacity 50%, Blur 0, Scale 200%, and Angle 0.

037 – THE REFLECTION SHADOW

The reflection shadow is rarely seen but is an interesting use of shadow that is perfect for some main titles. This title was created in Boris's Title 3D, which has an extensive variety of text shadow options.

Most applications don't include shadow controls to create this specific effect. However, it is easy to make from scratch using duplicate text and a mirror filter.

Duplicate the title and change the duplicate title's color to your desired shadow color. Apply a mirror filter to the duplicate and move the duplicate behind the original text so that only the mirrored portion below the original text is showing. Or you can just crop the top half of the mirrored text. Once the mirrored text is in position, lower the Opacity to around 75%.

038 – THE SPILLED SHADOW

The spilled shadow is an exaggerated shadow that creates the illusion of the shadow spilling out from below the text. Like some of the other rare but stylish shadow varieties, this can be effective for main titles, credits, and possibly interjections.

This example was created in Apple's LiveType application, which includes controls for stretching and distorting shadows. This effect can also be created by duplicating the text, changing the color and opacity of the duplicate, and modifying the scale and position. Consider exaggerating the long, lean title look by resizing the vertical (y) scale more than the horizontal (x).

SPILLED SHADOW

039 – THE CAST SHADOW

The cast shadow feels as if the shadow is being cast onto a horizontal surface rather than against the background. This title was created in Boris's Title 3D and utilizes the z axis to throw the shadow back into the distance. You can also create this look using duplicate text and modifying the duplicate's perspective, color, and opacity.

OUTLINE TECHNIQUES AND VARIATIONS

**OUTLINE SETUP
(APPLY TO PREPARED
BASIC TITLES)**

Requirements
Software
Any nonlinear editing or
motion graphics software
with title generator

Recommended Layout Features
None

*Software Titling Advanced
Features*
Outline feature or
Outline Text generator
with controls: blur, width,
opacity, and color

Time: 1–5 minutes

Preparation: Open a
project containing a basic
title. Select the text object
and turn on or apply the
outline feature. With some
applications, such as Final
Cut Pro, you must first
create the text using the
Outline Text title generator
before you can add and
manipulate the outline.

Another way to separate text from the background, or dress it up a
bit, is to add an outline. You can apply outlines lightly or apply them
more heavily to create distinctively different looks. Outlines are generally easy to apply and modify as needed. They are commonly used
on interjections, main titles, credits, and lower thirds. They are not
recommended for block text.

The techniques and variations in this section show plain white or
black text; however, you could substitute the black with any dark
color and substitute the white with any light or pastel color. You'll
find details about working with color in Chapter 3.

Opacity, Blur, and Width

Outlines are defined by four parameters: opacity, blur, width, and
color. These controls are fairly self-explanatory and work similarly
to the drop shadow, but with an outline there is no offset or distance
because an outline always borders the text.

You'll find full-resolution still images or QuickTime movies of
each example on the companion DVD included with this book. The
path is TITLE_DESIGN_ESSENTIALS > Chapter 2 > Outline.

Outline Checklist

Before you add an outline to your text, make sure you have a clear
understanding as to why you are adding it in the first place.

✔ Do you want to separate the text from the background?

✔ Does the text seem dull, lifeless, and need a little spicing up?

✔ Do you want to emphasize certain words and phrases?

TIP: If you are working with an application that does not have an outline text feature, you can create a similar effect by duplicating the text object. Place the duplicate
below the original text and make the duplicate several point sizes larger than the
original text. Change the color of the duplicate to the outline color. You can resize and
blur the duplicate text as needed to create the desired look.

040 – THE CLASSIC OUTLINE (AKA THE DEFAULT)

The classic outline is the most common outline look and adds a subtle border around the text. This outline style is the default setting for many applications when the feature is enabled, applied, or turned on.

The classic outline separates the text from the background (as long as it differs from the background color). It has a clean and conservative look suitable for any main title, lower third, credit, or interjection.

You can create a classic outline by setting the parameters to Width 1, Opacity 100%, and Blur 0.

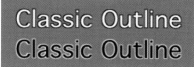

041 – THE DRAMATIC OUTLINE

The dramatic outline has a striking look, is more daring, and has an intense look like that of a movie star with stunning eyeliner. It works well with main titles, lower thirds, credits, and interjections.

Start with the classic outline, and then make the Width 2.

The dramatic outline settings are Width 2, Opacity 100%, and Blur 0.

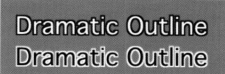

042 – THE HEAVY LIGHT OUTLINE

Heavy light isn't an oxymoron, although it could be mistaken for one. Actually, it is the use of a heavy outline on light (thin) text. The result is quite powerful and eye-catching. It is not ideal for the conservative project. This technique has a neon-like quality and is great for daring main titles, credits, and interjections.

Start with a narrow, light, or ultralight font, add a heavy outline, and then use the settings Width 3, Opacity 100%, and Blur 0.

043 – THE LIGHT AND FLUFFY OUTLINE

The light and fluffy outline is a variation of the light and heavy. The difference is the addition of a blur to give it a more diffused neon look.

Start with the heavy light outline settings of Width 3, Opacity 100%, and then add a Blur of 2.

044 – THE CLOUD OUTLINE

The cloud outline is similar to the cloud shadow except that the cloud outline surrounds the text in a heavier cloud. It is very handy for placing text over a busy background or texture. This technique is often seen in commercials with interjection text. It is occasionally used for main titles or credits.

To achieve this look, start with an extra heavy outline (Width 5–7) and then add a lot of Blur (10–30).

The cloud outline settings are Width 7, Opacity 100%, and Blur 10.

045 – THE SPRAYED OUTLINE

The sprayed outline is not your ordinary outline. The sprayed outline has a rough, spray painted look that works well for a stenciled, tagged feel. It could be used for either a main title or interjection. The secret to the sprayed outline is the use of a thick hand-written, wide, or stenciled font.

The sprayed outline settings are Width 8, Opacity 100%, and Blur 1.

046 – THE FACE–OFF OUTLINE

The face-off outline refers to the fact that the opacity of the face (text fill color) is lower than the opacity of the outline. The face-off technique can be used for main titles, lower thirds, credits, and interjections.

Simply create a text object with an outline the same color as the text. Then lower the opacity of the text while keeping the outline at 100%. This technique works best on bold style type.

The face-off outline settings are Width 2, Outline opacity 100%, Blur 0, and text face opacity 50–75%.

Text face opacity 75%

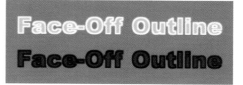

Text face opacity 50%

047 – THE HALF FACE OUTLINE

The half face outline is the opposite of the face-off outline. In this variation, the text face is at 100% opacity and the outline 50%. This adds a subtle twist to the dramatic outline. It's great for main titles, lower thirds, credits, and interjections.

The half face outline settings are Width 2, Outline opacity 50%, and Blur 0.

048 – THE TWO–TONED OUTLINE

The two-toned outline gets its name from mixing the text color and outline colors within a word, phrase, or sentence. Start by creating a classic or dramatic outline, and then alternate text color and outline color combinations. This technique is most commonly used in main titles, credits, and interjections.

The two-toned outline settings are Width 2, Outline opacity 100%, and Blur 0.

SHADOW AND OUTLINE COMBINATION TECHNIQUES

Sometimes, drop shadows or outlines are not enough on their own. In that case, you can combine them to really spice up your titles. These techniques are illustrated in both black and white text with the shadow and outline combinations in alternating black and white. The black-and-white color in the text, shadow, or outline can be substituted anytime with other light or dark colors. It's important to remember how the drop shadows and outlines work together to create a different text look.

You'll find full-resolution still images or QuickTime movies of each example on the companion DVD included with this book. The path is TITLE_DESIGN_ESSENTIALS > Chapter 2 > Shadow Outline Combinations.

049 – THE CLASSIC COMBO

As the name suggests, the classic combo uses the classic drop shadow with the classic outline. This clean and classy look can be used for conservative or fun projects. It's easy to read over any colored background and works for main titles, credits, lower thirds, and interjections.

Shadow settings are Distance 3–5, Blur 0, Opacity 75%, and Angle 315 degrees.

Outline settings are Width 1, Opacity 100%, and Blur 0.

050 – THE FORECOMBO

This forecombo technique is a combination of the classic outline and the foreshadow. The forecombo makes striking, easy to read text with a hint of a 3D feel because of the thick shadow preceding the text.

Shadow settings are Opacity 75%, Angle 180, and Distance 5.

Outline settings are Width 1, Opacity 100%, and Blur 0.

051 – THE AFTCOMBO

Similar to the forecombo, the aftcombo technique combines the classic outline with the aftshadow. This striking combo also has a unique 3D feel and works well over any color or textured background.

Shadow settings are Opacity 75%, Angle 0, and Distance 5.

Outline settings are Width 1, Opacity 100%, and Blur 0.

052 – THE CLASSIC FLUFFY COMBO

The classic fluffy combo is a blend of the classic drop shadow with a fluffy outline. The classic shadow gives the text crisp, stand-out edges, whereas the fluffy outline softens the overall look.

Shadow settings are Distance 3–5, Blur 0, Opacity 75%, and Angle 315 degrees.

Outline settings are Width 1–2, Opacity 100%, and Blur 2.

053 – THE DRAMATIC FLUFFY COMBO

The dramatic fluffy combo uses the dramatic outline with the fluffy drop shadow to create an overall dramatic look.

Shadow settings are Distance 3–5, Blur 2–3, Opacity 100%, and Angle 315 degrees.

Outline settings are Width 2, Opacity 100%, and Blur 0.

Shadow and Outline Combination Techniques

054 – THE LOOMING DRAMATIC COMBO

The looming dramatic combo uses two uniquely different styles to create an interesting look. Like the looming shadow, this combo works well for mystery, comedy, or horror title sequences.

Shadow settings are Distance 0, Opacity 50%, Blur 0, Scale 200%, and Angle 0.

Outline settings are Width 2, Opacity 100%, and Blur 0.

055 – THE DRAMATIC CLOUD COMBO

Guaranteed to help text stand out against any color or texture, the dramatic cloud combo utilizes the dramatic outline with the cloud shadow.

Shadow settings are Distance 0, Blur 20–30, Opacity 100%, and Scale 150%.

Outline settings are Width 2, Opacity 100%, and Blur 0.

GLOW TECHNIQUES AND VARIATIONS

Glows are less common than the drop shadow and outline. They add a luminescent glow that borders the text, similar to an outline. Glows are usually yellow or bright colors on dark text but can also be the reverse. Glows are not often found in editing applications but are available in graphics applications such as Motion, After Effects, and LiveType.

Glows are often animated for a luminous, glowing look.

These techniques show plain white or black text with a standard yellow glow over both black and gray backgrounds.

Radius and Offset

Glows are defined using color, opacity, blur, radius, scale, and offset. These controls are similar to those of outlines and drop shadows. The main differences are the radius and offset controls. Radius determines the circumference or how far the glow radiates around the text. This is similar to the width control for outlines. An offset control allows you to move the glow away from the text. This is similar to the distance control for drop shadow.

GLOW SETUP (APPLY TO PREPARED BASIC TITLES)

Requirements

Software
Any nonlinear editing or motion graphics software with title generator

Recommended Layout Features
None

Software Titling Advanced Features
Glow feature with controls: opacity, blur, radius, scale, offset, and color

Time: 1–5 minutes

Preparation: Open a project containing a basic title. Select the text object and turn on or apply the glow feature.

You'll find full-resolution still images or QuickTime movies of each example on the companion DVD included with this book. The path is TITLE_DESIGN_ESSENTIALS > Chapter 2 > Glows.

Glow Checklist

Before you add glow to your text, consider these questions.

✔ Do you want to separate the text from the background?

✔ Does the text seem dull, lifeless, and need a little spicing up?

✔ Do you want the text to radiate a color or seem illuminated from behind?

✔ Do you want to emphasize certain words and phrases with the use of a glow?

NOTE: If your application does not include a glow feature, you can achieve a similar look with a fluffy yellow outline.

056 – THE CLASSIC GLOW

The classic glow is the lightest glow setting and creates a barely discernable glow behind the text. As you can see in the image, this glow works better on dark text. This technique can be used to create subtle main titles or credits.

The classic glow settings are Opacity 100%, Blur 1, Radius 3, Scale 100%, and Offset 0.

057 – THE MEDIUM GLOW

A medium glow is the most common glow and is similar to the dramatic outline. It is very effective for separating the text from the background. This style is often used to spice up interjections in commercials. It can also be found in main titles and credits.

The medium glow settings are Opacity 100%, Blur 1, Radius 50, Scale 100%, and Offset 0.

058 – THE HEAVY GLOW

The heavy glow is a bit too much for most situations but has its moments, such as an interjection over a dark background or an action main title over a fast-paced video background.

Start with a medium glow, and then add more radius and blur to taste.

The heavy glow settings are Opacity 100%, Blur 2, Radius 100, Scale 100%, and Offset 0.

059 – THE FLUFFY GLOW

The fluffy glow is similar to the fluffy outline and shadows. The main difference is that the other fluffy variations are soft and elegant. This glow radiates like text on fire or text steeped in nuclear waste. Although it's not pretty to look at, these titles work for eye-catching interjections and titles that demand attention. It may not win any design awards, but you'll definitely get attention.

The heavy glow settings are Opacity 100%, Blur 3, Radius 51, Scale 100%, and Offset 0.

CHAPTER 3

Enhancing Text with Color and Gradients

Color is an excellent way to dress up your text whether you enhance it with a subtle touch of color or embellish it with a brightly colored gradient. Color and gradients can be used to make an impression beyond the content of the text. They can also be used to emphasize words, phrases, or sentences. Best of all, color and gradients can add a professional look to the text that can't be achieved any other way. Just as an interior designer uses colorful paints, prints, and accents to complete the look of a room, in this chapter you'll see a sample of techniques for adding colorful accents to your text.

Working with Color

As children, we are introduced to simple colors like red, yellow, and blue. Eventually we work our way up to the big box of crayons. Even with all the colors available, designers tend to use the primary and secondary colors more often than others. Why? These colors have strong meanings in our everyday lives that we perceive without even thinking about them.

Red has powerful negative connotations such as stop, warning, danger, and biohazard. Even in nature red-colored bands or spots on creatures such as ants, frogs, or snakes indicate a warning against poison or danger. When people in most cultures see a sign with red letters or letters on a red background, they assume it is some kind of warning.

Red holds such a strong negative impact that you will rarely ever see a person's name written in red letters. Imagine a political campaign commercial with the candidate's name in big red letters. It may look impressive and be eye-catching, but viewers will likely sense it as a warning even if they like that particular candidate. If you see a name in red in a political commercial, it is usually the opponent's name.

An exception is if red is part of a company logo or insignia. Then the red color is part of the company's identity and will not be interpreted as a warning.

Another exception is if the text colors correspond with the colors of a flag, such as red, white, and blue. Then the red would seem patriotic rather than a warning.

NOTE: The use of a fluffy outline or shadow softens the text to give it extra emphasis and makes it feel friendlier. Italicized text also has a kinder, more personable feeling.

The only other exception for red is love. If words or phrases are bright red or on a red background and involve romance or valentines, the accepted meaning is love or some kind of romantic message. Adding cupids, hearts, and flowers helps amplify the meaning, but love works in any color, especially red.

Red is ideal for main titles that invoke a feeling of danger, horror (blood), action, and love or romance.

Green is the color of money, wisdom, and "Go" in traffic situations. Even in speech, if a project gets a "green light," it means go ahead. Green is positive but not universally used except in reference to money. Banks and lending institutions use green in their signage or commercial text, but white text is more common and institutional.

Green is used for the main titles of documentaries or projects with environmental "green" themes. It is also associated with aliens (little green men), space, and science fiction projects in both the main titles and the credits.

Yellow is generally used for caution, attention, or to explain why you need to be cautious or pay special attention. Text in yellow means read me first or pay attention to me (unless there is red text, which demands more attention than yellow).

It is trendy to use yellow in short blocks of text to emphasize key words or phrases.

Yellow is also used in interjections to grab attention or to explain why a product, company, or place is best.

Since yellow means caution, it also is associated with adventure and excitement. You'll find yellow (solid or gradient) in the main titles and credits of popular action and adventure films and shows.

Blue is the universal calm, cool, and collected color. Perhaps because the sky is blue and the ocean is blue, but generally, blue is gentle and peaceful on the eyes. Doctors' and dentists' offices often use blue with beige or white to give the office or patient rooms a more welcoming feel. Signs for congratulations, happy birthday, and have a nice day are often blue with white or yellow trim. Ironically, when people say they feel blue, they refer to being sad, yet blue text means the opposite.

Where red means "warning" or "danger" and yellow means "caution," blue feels more like "Hello, how are you today?" Titles that list changes or new policies seem less intrusive if they are accompanied by blue text rather than any other color.

If you are emphasizing a person's name, a place, or a company name, blue feels more welcoming, accessible, and trustworthy.

Which feels more inviting and trustworthy at a glance?

Blue is used for the main titles and credits of drama, comedy, and family-oriented projects. If it is a feel-good project, there's a good chance the title has blue in the vicinity. Blue is also associated with magic or supernatural powers.

NOTE: Some projects use a color opposite of the project or title's theme or meaning just to play with the audience's expectations. For example, a film about a town full of vampires might use a welcoming blue in the titles to set the tone that the place is normal and peaceful, only to surprise the audience with the first bloodletting. A red title would be the obvious choice in this scenario but lacks the element of surprise.

Primary and Secondary Colors

Now that you've seen which colors have a strong underlying meaning, let's look at the primary and secondary colors over dark, medium, and light backgrounds.

The primary colors are red, yellow, and blue. Depending on which two of the primary colors you mix, you'll get the secondary colors orange, green, and purple.

One consideration in selecting a color, aside from its meaning, is how it will look on top of the background. Titles are most often created on black or dark backgrounds; however, a background can also be medium or light in color.

NOTE: You'll find more specific information on backgrounds in Chapter 5, "Creating Project-based Titles."

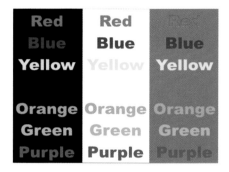

Text that uses primary or secondary colors usually looks best over two of the three tonal ranges (dark, medium, or light). Blue, orange, and green stand out best over all three types of backgrounds.

Using color for only the text outline or shadow works really well with dark colors on light backgrounds and light colors on dark backgrounds.

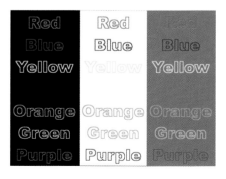

Complementary Colors

Colors at opposite sides of the color wheel are referred to as complementary colors because they make both colors appear brighter when placed next to each other.

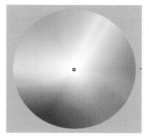

Mac OS X Color Wheel

You can find the complementary color of any primary color by mixing the other two primary colors.

The complementary color for red is green, blue is orange, and yellow is purple.

These complementary color pairs are associated with holidays, sports teams, flags, and company logos because they work so well together.

As you can see in the illustration, text that uses complementary colors is easy to read over dark, light, or medium backgrounds.

TITLE COLOR TECHNIQUES AND VARIATIONS

TITLE COLOR SETUP (APPLY TO PREPARED BASIC TITLES)

Requirements

Software
Any nonlinear editing or motion graphics software with title generator

Recommended Layout Features
Text face color controls

Software Titling Advanced Features
Outline controls including color

Drop shadow controls including color

Time: 1–5 minutes

Preparation: Open a project containing a basic title. Select the text object and turn on or apply color to the face, outline, or shadow as needed.

Selecting a color is like painting your text. Choose the color wisely and keep in mind that a little bit of colored text goes a long way in your titles. Just like fonts, too many colors will look distracting and unprofessional.

You can add color to any of the previous variations in this book. Here is a sampling of some common uses of color in titles. Keep in mind that you can substitute any color and mix and match colors to best fit your projects.

You'll find full-resolution still images or QuickTime movies on the companion DVD included with this book. The path is TITLE_ DESIGN_ESSENTIALS > Chapter 3 > Color.

Title Color Checklist

Before you add color to your text, consider these points.

✔ Do you want to emphasize certain words or phrases with the use of color?

✔ Do you want to add underlying meaning to titles with the use of color?

✔ Are you working over a light, medium, or dark background? You'll want to choose a color, outline, or shadow that stands out well against that background.

NOTE: If you've never added color to the text, shadow, or outline using your software, take a moment to familiarize yourself with those features before moving on to the title color variations.

060 – BOLD AND BRIGHT

Using bold and bright colors helps emphasize text to make a strong statement. A bold font style and large text also accentuate the tone. This style looks good over any shade of background and can be used as a warning or caution, or simply to capture attention. This technique is used in main titles, credits, lower thirds, and interjections.

NOTE: Using bold and capitalized letters is the text equivalent of yelling or screaming. Bright colors such as yellow or red may add a certain tone, such as danger, warning, caution, or attention.

061 – SOFT AND SUBTLE

Soft and subtle text colors include all pastel colors and have the opposite effect of bold and bright colors. Soft and subtle colors are like a whisper, secret, or suggestion. These colors often accompany handwriting fonts or thin italicized font styles. This style is used for main titles, credits, or interjections intended to be less obvious.

062 – SHADOW COLOR

The shadow color technique applies a color instead of black, white, or gray for a title's drop shadow. This is one of the most common uses of color in titles and is widely used in main titles, credits, lower thirds, interjections, and key information text. Colored drop shadows work with black, white, or colored text.

TIP: If you're not sure which color to choose for your text's shadow, try a complementary color, or the color to the right or left of the complementary color on the color wheel. Also try using dark colors with light colored text or light colors with dark colored text.

063 – OUTLINE COLOR

Outline color can be applied to any of the outline variations. An outline color works great over any background shade, or text. This technique is used for main titles, credits, lower thirds, and interjections.

NOTE: When adding a colored outline to colored text, keep in mind that the viewer will perceive the separate colors but may also see the combined color. In the following example, the red text with the yellow outline has an orange feel at a glance, even though there is no orange used in the text.

064 – ALTERNATING BLACK AND WHITE COLOR COMBOS

You can add a twist to the outline/shadow combo variations by adding a color to the outline. This technique gives the text definition and a unique three-dimensional quality that can't be achieved any other way. This technique works best with dark color outlines over backgrounds that don't match the drop shadow.

Start with a classic combo and add a dark color to the outline.

The alternating black, white, and color titles come in four variations: white text, color outline, white drop shadow; black text, color outline, black drop shadow; black text, color outline, white shadow; and white text, color outline, black shadow.

This technique employs a conservative use of color and adds a bit of flair to titles without over doing it. Modify the outline and shadow parameters to taste.

065 – TRI–COLOR TEXT

As the name suggests, tri-color text includes a combination of three different colors for the face, outline, and shadow. This technique works equally well with light or dark colored text and adds a fun and contemporary look to titles. It's perfect for interjections, main titles, credits, or lower thirds.

This variation works as an embellishment for any of the shadow/outline combo variations.

066 – TRI–COLOR SHADES

Tri-color shades is a more conservative spin on the tri-color text. Tri-color shades applies three different shades of the same color to the text. Start with a classic combo variation, and then add color to the text. Once you've selected a text color, choose a darker or lighter shade of the same color to apply to the outline and a different shade for the drop shadow. This style works for main titles, credits, interjections, and lower thirds.

Adjust the outline and shadow parameters to taste.

Working with Gradients

Two or more colors that gradually blend from one to another are referred to as gradients. Gradients are used as backgrounds and also in text. Solid color text is effective and easy to read. However, gradient color text draws emphasis in a more decorative way. Gradients are like text wallpaper. A little goes a long way, and too much can be gaudy and distracting. Gradients are commonly seen in company logos, company names, main titles, credits, and lower thirds. Gradients have a richer feel than plain colored text and if used sparingly can really enhance text to give it a high-quality, professional look.

Types of Gradients

Gradients don't require a color, they can be black and white with a grayscale in the middle. There are many different types of gradients with countless possible combinations of direction, colors, and shades. Gradients are described by the number of colors and the direction in which the colors blend from one to the next.

Most of the gradients used in titles are two-toned with white or black and follow a horizontal direction. They can also follow a vertical, diagonal, or radial direction, although this is rarely used in text.

NOTE: All of these examples work as is or flopped 180 degrees with the gradient moving in the opposite direction.

Horizontal white and color   *Horizontal black and color*   *Vertical white and color*

Gradients can also have a diagonal or radial direction.

Diagonal complementary

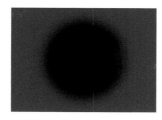

Radial black and color

Radial color and color

Complementary colors can be used in two-toned gradients or mixed in a splash of white or black to create a tri-colored complementary gradient.

Complementary colors

Complementary with white

Complementary with black

Tri-colored gradients can be any three colors. Tri-color shades gradients use three shades of the same color.

Tri-color gradient

Tri-color shades

TITLE GRADIENT TECHNIQUES AND VARIATIONS

TITLE GRADIENT SETUP (APPLY TO PREPARED BASIC TITLES)

Requirements

Software
  Any nonlinear editing or motion graphics software with title generator

Recommended Layout Features
  Text face color controls

Software Titling Advanced Features
  Gradient generator or gradient controls

  Outline controls including color

  Drop shadow controls including color

Time: 3–8 minutes; Gradients may take a little more time to apply than color because you first need to create the gradient.

Preparation: Open a project containing a basic title. Select the text object and turn on or apply a gradient face color. Adjust the gradient colors and direction as needed.

You can add gradients to any of the previous variations in this book. Here is a sampling of some useful title gradients. Keep in mind that you can substitute any color and mix and match colors to create gradients that better fit your project.

You'll find full-resolution still images or QuickTime movies on the companion DVD included with this book. The path is TITLE_DESIGN_ESSENTIALS > Chapter 3 > Gradients.

Title Gradient Checklist

Before you add a gradient to your text, consider these points.

✔ Do you want to emphasize certain words or phrases with the use of a gradient?

✔ Do you want to decorate some of your titles to make them appear more important, attractive, or eye-catching?

✔ Do you want the text to stand out from the background?

NOTE: Some applications, such as Final Cut Pro, include separate text and gradient generators. If your application doesn't allow you to apply a gradient directly to the text through the text controls, create the gradient separately and add it to the text using an alpha traveling matte. You'll find more information about composite modes or adding gradients to text in your application's documentation. Take a few minutes to familiarize yourself with your application's gradient features before continuing on with the variations.

067 – WHITE AND COLOR GRADIENT

The white and color gradient is the most widely used text gradient variation. Simply create a horizontal gradient with white and your color of choice, and then apply it to the text. This technique is clean and professional looking with a friendly, positive feel that works great for main titles, credits, interjections, and lower thirds. White and color gradients work best over backgrounds that are not white.

068 – BLACK AND COLOR GRADIENT

The black and color gradient is another common gradient style. Simply create a horizontal gradient with black and your color of choice, and then apply it to the text. This type of gradient is also clean and professional looking but has a more stern, serious, or dramatic feel. Try this technique for serious main titles, credits, interjections, and lower thirds. Black and color gradients work best over backgrounds that are not black.

069 – VERTICAL GRADIENT

Rarely used in text, the vertical gradient has a unique artistic feel. Try this variation with black and color for a more serious feel, white and color for a lighter feel, or two colors. Since vertical gradients emphasize each letter of a word rather than the entire word or statement, they are very effective for acronyms and short titles.

070 – DIAGONAL GRADIENT

The diagonal gradient is another artistic option for the text gradient. It can be subtle or dramatic depending on the colors within the gradient. If it is a soft, two-color gradient, the diagonal feels more like a delicate shading or accent. If you use a strong tri-color or multi-color gradient, the diagonal direction will be more visible.

Title Gradient Techniques and Variations

071 – RADIAL GRADIENT

Radial gradients have a circular pattern that radiates out from the center. These gradients are used more often as backgrounds than in text. Applying a radial gradient to text emphasizes the individual letters. Using a light color in the center of the gradient gives the text the appearance that it is illuminated from within, whereas using the lighter color on the outside of the gradient will make the text appear to be illuminated from the outside. Text with radial gradients are most effective for interjections.

072 – COMPLEMENTARY COLOR GRADIENT

If you're looking for a gradient that stands out on any background, try using complementary colors. You can combine two complementary colors or add black or white in the middle. Remember, white will seem light and friendly; black will seem more serious.

NOTE: The upside to using complementary colors in text is that the colors are combinations that are already familiar and recognizable for flags, holidays, sports teams, and logos. The downside is that they are recognizable for flags, holidays, sports teams, and logos. In other words, this technique can work for you or against you depending on the situation. If you choose colors used by the hometown college football team and you're a local advertiser, go for it. Or if you're making titles for an upcoming holiday like Christmas or Easter, they'll fit right in.

073 – TRI–SHADES GRADIENT

The tri-shades gradients are tasteful and pretty to look at, and can really make text look decorative. This technique works beautifully with main titles, credits, interjections, and lower thirds.

074 – TRI–COLOR GRADIENT

You can liven up your text with a tri-color gradient. Tri-colors can add a festive look, show off company colors, or simply demand attention. These can be tasteful or gaudy but are always effective, especially with main titles and interjections.

075 – SHADOW LIGHT/DARK GRADIENT

If you want to spice up your gradients, add a colorful drop shadow. The shadow light gradient technique uses the light color in the gradient as the drop shadow color. The shadow dark gradient utilizes the darker gradient color for the drop shadow. Both techniques are tasteful and add dimension to the text in an eye-pleasing way.

Start with classic shadow text, add the gradient to the face color, and choose one of the gradient colors for the drop shadow.

076 – OUTLINE LIGHT/DARK GRADIENT

Another way to spice up your gradient text is to match an outline to the light or dark color in the gradient. This technique adds a colorful and professional-looking edge to main titles, interjections, and lower thirds text.

Feel free to adjust the outline width to taste.

TIP: The shadow light/dark and outline light/dark gradient variations also work great with black and white gradients.

Title Gradient Techniques and Variations

CHAPTER 4

Working with Basic Animation

In this book, animation refers to changes to a parameter over time such as scale, opacity, or position. Titles can also be hand drawn and animated like cartoon characters, but that is a different type of animation—and a different book entirely.

Virtually any text property from scale to color can be animated. In this chapter I'll illustrate the four most common and useful elements for title animation: opacity, scale, tracking, and position. Opacity animation creates fades and dissolves. Scale animation creates changes in text size to grow or shrink titles. Tracking animation pulls letters closer together or pushes them farther apart. Position animation moves text. These animation techniques work well individually, but combined they can create even more powerful animation such as text that fades in as it grows and the tracking loosens.

To start, it is a good idea to understand why titles are animated in the first place. There are several reasons. Animation provides a professional-looking entrance and exit for titles. For example, titles can fade in, move in, or track into frame, stay for a while, and then exit with a fade out, move out, or track out of frame. Animation also gives titles movement that attracts the viewer's attention more than any other titling strategy.

Design Strategy to Emphasize Specific Words or Phrases

Drawing attention to specific words or phrases onscreen involves design strategy and an understanding of the different techniques in order of their effectiveness. Here is a list of design strategies in order of perceived importance.

1. Animated text (fades rank lowest for animation; moving and scaling text rank highest)

2. Colored text, especially bright, bold colors (yellow and red attract the most attention; red trumps yellow)

3. Shadow/outline combinations

4. Outlined text (dramatic, heavy, or fluffy outlines trump a classic outline)

5. Text with drop shadows (foreshadow, aftshadow, looming, and spilled shadows trump the classic drop shadow and classic outline)

6. Bold fonts or text larger than any other text onscreen at the same time

7. All fonts, scale, styles, and color the same onscreen—all text is considered of equal importance

The higher the strategy is in the list, the more effective the design technique. For example, bold text has more presumed value than regular text, but colored text trumps the bold text, and zooming text trumps all other text onscreen at the same time.

This strategy list only works if some words, phrases, or sentences have been treated with different techniques in the list. If all text onscreen at the same time appears the same (even animated), then all of the text has the same presumed importance to the viewer.

Animating Opacity: Fades and Cross Dissolves

Two of the simplest and most commonly used forms of title animation are fades and dissolves. These are created by animating the opacity of a title. Opacity refers to how opaque (solid) an object appears. If an object has an opacity value of 100 percent, it has zero transparency. Zero percent opacity means that an object is 100 percent transparent (invisible). Animating opacity is used to create either a fade or dissolve effect.

Working with Fades

The lights of a movie theater slowly dim before the start of a movie and gradually brighten at the end of the movie. This effect is also referred to as fading the lights up or down. If the lights just went out suddenly, the audience's eyes wouldn't have time to adjust to the dark, and if the lights suddenly came on after the movie, the audience would have to shade its eyes or squint from the sudden onset of bright light. Fading the lights is a courtesy to make the change in light more gradual and comfortable.

Fading titles in and out is similar to the theater lights in that the title appears and disappears gradually. This technique is also a courtesy to the audience because the fade in is a polite way for the title to appear as if it is saying "Hello, would you like to read me?" The fade out is a polite exit as if it is saying "Goodbye, thanks for reading me." The fade out could also mean "read faster" because the title is leaving. Either way it is more courteous than the title just disappearing.

Fade effects are used to make objects appear or disappear into the background. They are also referred to as transitions because they offer a transition from no title to the title onscreen. Fades are created by increasing the opacity value of a title to create a fade in or decreasing its opacity value to create a fade out.

Fades are the most commonly used animation effect in professional titles and can be used with any type of title on any type of project. Not only are they a classy and graceful way for text to make an appearance onscreen, but they are also very easy effects to create.

The speed of fades can vary from a slow fade that takes several seconds until the object is fully opaque to a swift fade where the object blinks on in a fraction of a second. In both cases the look is different than if the object just appears onscreen without any fade at all.

There are three primary considerations when creating basic fades:

- The speed (duration) of the fade in

- The speed (duration) of the fade out

- The length of time you want the text onscreen

Determining the speed of the fade in and out can be based on the style or feel of a project, or based on necessity if you have a limited amount of time to show the titles. Fast fades have a more energetic, active look and feel. They are also more likely to catch viewers' attention than a slow and gradual fade. Slow fades, on the other hand, have a more graceful, calm, thoughtful feel. An extreme sports show may have very fast fading titles that go with the overall action-packed feel of the project. A commercial for a bank or dramatic movie may have slow fading titles for a more stable, conservative, and unhurried feel.

The formula for holding text onscreen depends on whether viewers are actually supposed to read the text or not. If the intention is for them to read it, the text should be onscreen long enough for a fast reader to read it three times or a slow reader to read it once. If it is a big text block that is onscreen to fulfill a legal obligation and isn't intended to actually be read, a few seconds onscreen will due.

Animating a List

If you want to animate a list so that one item appears at a time to build the list, you could create each item in the list as a separate text object. The downside to using this method is that you have to be very careful when placing each item in the list onscreen so that it is aligned properly in the list. Instead, you can build the entire list, and then duplicate the completed list text object as many times as there are items in the list. Delete list items from the different duplicate text objects until each duplicate has a different number of items in the list, starting with an empty list and building to the full list. Arrange the text objects in your editing or motion graphics software so that the title with an empty list is first, followed by the list with one item, then two items, and so on. Add a cross dissolve transition between each of the text objects or overlap them with fade transitions so that one item appears at a time in the list when the final animation is played.

Working with Cross Dissolves

In the movie theater scenario, if the exit lights became brighter as the house lights were fading out, that would simulate the visual effect of a cross dissolve.

Cross dissolves are really two fades happening simultaneously. One object fades in while the other fades out. This type of animated transition is referred to as a cross dissolve because the images cross each other onscreen as one is disappearing and the other appearing. Unlike fades that affect only one object at a time, cross dissolves raise the opacity of one object while lowering the opacity of another.

Cross dissolves are commonly used with credits, list text, and lower thirds to add new text to existing text on the screen.

Cross dissolves are useful for fading one title out while the other title fades in. This works well if the titles are in different positions on the screen, like the credits in the following example.

Cross dissolving from one piece of text to another in the same position onscreen can look messy and very unprofessional because both titles seemingly collide when they are visible at the same time during the effect.

TITLE OPACITY ANIMATION TECHNIQUES AND VARIATIONS

TITLE OPACITY ANIMATION SETUP (APPLY TO PREPARED BASIC TITLES)

Requirements

Software
   Any nonlinear editing or motion graphics software with title generator

Recommended Layout Features
   Opacity controls

Software Titling Advanced Features
   Keyframe or animation controls to change opacity values over time

   Optional: premade, modifiable fade or cross dissolve effects

Time: 1–5 minutes

Preparation: Open a project containing a basic title. Select the text object and turn on or apply changes to the text opacity values as needed.

Animating a title's opacity is an effective way to make text appear or disappear onscreen. Fades and dissolves can be added to any of the previous title techniques described in this book. Here is a sampling of some common fades and dissolves used in title animation. Keep in mind that you can vary the duration of the fades and dissolves to create different variations to better fit your projects.

All fades and dissolves with 100 percent opacity changes look the same. The only element that really differs is the speed of the fade, which is controlled by the duration. In most cases the duration of a fade in matches the duration of the fade out on the same title.

You'll find full-resolution still images or QuickTime movies on the companion DVD included with this book. The path is TITLE_DESIGN_ESSENTIALS > Chapter 4 > Opacity.

Title Opacity Animation Checklist

Before you add fades or dissolves to your text, consider these points.

✔ Do you want the text to make a smooth and gradual appearance?

✔ What is the overall tone or feel of the project? Consider quick fades for more energetic titles and slow fades for more conservative projects.

✔ How long do you want to hold the text onscreen before fading it out?

✔ Do you have a limited amount of time to keep the text onscreen? If so, consider a faster fade to maximize the time the title is fully opaque onscreen.

✔ Is there already a title in the position onscreen where you'll be adding the new title? Will the new title replace the content of the old title? If so, consider fading out the first title, and then fading in the new one. If the new title is text that needs to be added to the text already onscreen, fade in the new text without changing the old text. If the new title contains the other text in the same position plus new information, you'll want to dissolve from the old text to the new text.

NOTE: If you've never modified text opacity, take a moment to familiarize yourself with that feature before moving on to the title opacity animation techniques. Most editing software includes prebuilt fade and cross dissolve transitions. You can also animate opacity manually by adding keyframes to set the opacity value changes over time.

077 – CLASSIC FADE/DISSOLVE

The classic fade in transition takes one full second to fade from 0 percent opacity to 100 percent. The classic fade out transition also takes one full second to go from 100 percent opacity to 0 percent. The classic cross dissolve takes one second for the outgoing title to fade to 0 percent opacity while the incoming title fades up to 100 percent. One second fades and cross dissolves are used for all types of titles and are often the default fade or cross dissolve transition length found in editing software, such as Final Cut Pro, with prebuilt transitions. You can use classic fades or cross dissolves for any type of title or project.

The classic fade/dissolve uses a duration of 1 second (30 frames NTSC, 25 frames PAL, 24 frames film).

0 frames NTSC

10 frames NTSC

20 frames NTSC

30 frames NTSC

078 – SLOW FADE/DISSOLVE

As the name suggests, slow fades and cross dissolves are longer and slower than classic fades. The relaxed feel of the slow fades work well with main titles for dramatic, heavy, or sentimental projects such movies, documentaries, or wedding videos.

The slow fade/dissolve technique uses a duration of 1.5–3 seconds (this example shows 2.5 seconds, 75 frames NTSC).

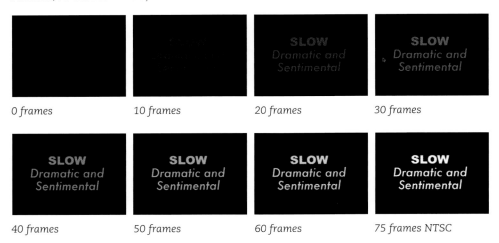

| *0 frames* | *10 frames* | *20 frames* | *30 frames* |

| *40 frames* | *50 frames* | *60 frames* | *75 frames NTSC* |

079 – LINGERING FADE/DISSOLVE

Lingering fades and cross dissolves deliver sentimentality and melodrama. However, they also can be used to emphasize a point that the audience may resist, dismiss, or ignore otherwise. These lingering transitions can be very effective for public service announcements, political commercials, documentaries, or emotional projects with titles containing facts and statements you want the audience to read and digest. Text that appears and disappears in a lingering fashion somehow seems less direct to an audience and more like a thought or suggestion. If the exact same text appears quickly, it may seem too direct or manipulative and turn off audiences.

The lingering fade/dissolve technique uses a duration of 3–8+ seconds (this example shows 4 seconds, 120 frames NTSC).

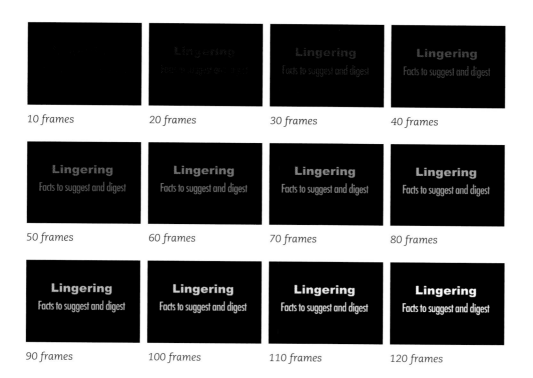

10 frames
20 frames
30 frames
40 frames

50 frames
60 frames
70 frames
80 frames

90 frames
100 frames
110 frames
120 frames

080 – FAST FADE/DISSOLVE

Fast fades are a great way to speed up titles, especially when you have a lot of text to fit into a short amount of time. These fades are also perfect for upbeat, energetic projects.

The fast fade/dissolve technique uses a duration of .5 seconds (15 frames NTSC, 12 frames PAL and film).

0 frames NTSC
7 frames NTSC
15 frames NTSC

081 – SWIFT FADE/DISSOLVE (AKA SOFT CUT)

Swift fades and dissolves are so fast they are barely visible. These are handy for titles that you want to appear or disappear in a hurry without having them pop in and out as a straight cut. Swift fades are also referred to as soft cuts because they offer a gentler transition in and out of a title than a cut. These illusive fades are fractions of a second but make a big difference in the overall feel of titles. When you have to bring in a lot of separate titles or blocks of text in a short amount of time, the swift fades offer a nice alternative to cuts without wasting precious screen time with lengthier transitions.

The swift fade/dissolve technique uses a duration of 3–6 frames for NTSC, PAL, and film. (This example is 4 frames NTSC.)

2 frames   4 frames

082 – MIXED SPEED FADE IN/FADE OUT

Occasionally, a title needs to fade in at a different speed than it fades out. This generally happens when titles are timed to music or choreographed to other action on the screen. Sometimes titles fade in slowly then fade out fast once the viewer has had a chance to read it. This helps clear away one title quickly to make room for another. The mixed speed fade in/fade out durations vary.

083 – PARTIAL FADE/DISSOLVE

A partial fade means the transition never reaches 100 percent opacity. This technique helps deemphasize text. If a title needs to appear but not compete with other text, fade it in to between 60 and 80 percent, and it will be clearly legible without the same crisp opacity as the other text. A partial fade is useful for disclaimers and short statements or blurbs. This technique also works for main titles and credits if understating the text is part of the overall design. The partial fade/dissolve durations vary.

60% opacity   80% opacity

Animating Scale

Changing a title's scale over time can create a zooming effect or make titles appear to be moving closer or farther away. Scale animation can also be used for more subtle scale changes, to grow or shrink text, or simply to add movement to draw attention to the title.

Scale changes are often used with interjection text in commercials, on key information text like phone numbers, and for main titles and credits. Animating scale is a guaranteed attention grabber and adds excitement and energy to otherwise lifeless text.

The speed of scale animation can vary from a slow constant change that appears to grow or shrink gracefully to a fast zooming effect where the text appears to rush toward the viewer or fly in from behind the camera toward the screen. In both cases the look is eye-catching and adds movement without changing the text's position on the screen.

There are five primary considerations when animating scale:

■ The ideal size of the text in the title design layout

■ The starting scale of the text

■ The ending scale of the text

■ The speed of the scale change

■ The length of time you want the text onscreen

When determining the starting or ending scale of the text, you simply need to decide if the text will start at its ideal size and then get larger or smaller, or if it will start at a large or small size and grow or shrink to the correct size. Whether you decide to have a scale change that leads to the desired size or away from the desired size, the important factor is to know the ideal size of the text before you start animating the scale.

The speed at which the scale changes can greatly affect the feel of the text. A slow, creeping scale change has a subtle growing or shrinking feel, whereas a rapid scale change feels more like a quick-zooming effect. How fast the scale change will occur is also contingent on how long the text will be onscreen and whether the scale change starts and stops or is continuous.

TITLE SCALE ANIMATION TECHNIQUES AND VARIATIONS

TITLE SCALE ANIMATION SETUP (APPLY TO PREPARED BASIC TITLES)

Requirements

Software
Any nonlinear editing or motion graphics software with title generator

Recommended Layout Features
Text size or scale controls

Software Titling Advanced Features
Keyframe or animation controls to change size/scale values over time

Optional: prebuilt zooming or scaling effects or transitions

Time: 1–5 minutes

Preparation: Open a project containing a basic title. Select the text object and turn on or apply changes to the text scale or point size values as needed.

Animating scale can be used as a transition to make text appear or disappear, to add a sense of visual movement toward or away from the screen, or simply to make the text seem more active. Here are some common scale animation techniques that are used with titles, especially main titles, credits, and interjections.

Each technique can be created at different speeds ranging from slow to rapid. Feel free to vary the duration and extent of the scale changes to better fit your projects.

You'll find full-resolution still images or QuickTime movies on the companion DVD included with this book. The path is TITLE_DESIGN_ESSENTIALS > Chapter 4 > Scale.

Title Scale Animation Checklist

Before you add scale animation to your text, consider these points.

✔ Do you want the text to appear or disappear into the background?

✔ What is the overall tone or feel of the project? Consider quick drastic scale changes to create zooms for more energetic titles or slow subtle scale changes for more conservative titles.

✔ Do you want the scale change to grow or shrink the text?

✔ Do you want the scale change to lead to the final text size or away from the final text size?

✔ How long do you want to hold the text onscreen without the scale changing?

✔ Do you want a continuous scale change while the text is onscreen?

✔ Do you have a limited amount of time to keep the text onscreen? If so, consider a faster scale change to maximize the time the title is at its intended size onscreen.

NOTE: If you've never modified text size before, take a moment to familiarize yourself with that feature before moving on to the title scale animation techniques. Some editing software includes prebuilt scale zooming or grow/shrink transitions and effects. You can also animate scale manually by adding keyframes to set the size or scale value changes over time.

Text Point Size Versus Scale Animation

Most professional applications offer two ways to animate the size of text. You can change the point size of the text over time or change the scale of the text object, just as you would a video clip or graphic. The difference is that point size changes work with the different sizes of the fonts installed on your computer. Scale changes to the object may simply stretch or shrink the text at the existing size. Check the documentation for your application to see how the different size or scaling controls affect text.

084 – SCALE IN/SCALE OUT (TRANSITIONS)

You can use the scale in/scale out technique as a transition to introduce text by having it grow from zero scale to the intended size. A fast scale in effect is very eye-catching and commonly found in commercials for key information and interjections.

085 – SCALE OUT (TRANSITION)

The scale out transition is an interesting way for text to disappear by shrinking into the distance. This technique is often used in commercials and works well as a companion effect to the scale in effect.

086 – GROWING TEXT

Text that grows while onscreen seems alive and is much more interesting than static text. This technique is often used for important names or catchy phrases in movie trailers. Growing text is also used in commercials with interjections and key information text. Main titles might also use growing text to make the title seem like it is moving toward the audience and growing in importance as well.

Growing text can be in constant motion so that it never stops growing for the duration of the time the title is onscreen. The effect can also be animated so that the text grows to the intended size and holds or starts at the intended size and then grows.

087 – SHRINKING TEXT

Text that slowly shrinks seems to be moving away. This technique can add life to text; however, the audience may also perceive text that moves away as losing importance.

Like growing text, shrinking text can be in constant motion so that it never stops shrinking for the duration of the time the title is onscreen. The effect can also be animated so that the text shrinks to the intended size and holds or starts by holding the intended size and then shrinking.

088 – ZOOMING IN

The zooming in effect starts with the text at a very large size (300% or more) and then shrinks it down to the intended size. This effect looks like the text is flying in from behind the camera and landing on the screen.

Add a fade in and attraction tracking animation to enhance the zooming or flying effect.

089 – ZOOMING OUT

The companion to the zooming in effect is the zooming out effect. By animating the scale so that it grows large (300% or more), it gives the text the appearance of zooming away or flying off the screen toward the audience or camera.

Add a fade out and repelling tracking animation to fade out and expand the text for a more powerful zooming out effect.

Tracking Animation

Another common title animation technique is to animate the tracking to move letters closer or farther apart over time. This effect is less common than the fades and scale changes but can be very effective in adding movement and life to text. Tracking changes are most often found in movie trailers, main titles for movies or television shows, or in commercials for interjections and pertinent key information text.

Like the other animation techniques, the speed of the tracking change can vary, as well as the amount of change.

There are five primary considerations when animating tracking:

- The ideal tracking value for the text

- The starting tracking value

- The ending tracking value

- The speed of the tracking change

- The length of time you want the text onscreen

Like the text scale animation, you also need to determine the starting and ending tracking values of the text, as well as if it will start animated, end animated, hold at some point, or change continuously.

The speed at which the tracking changes also affects the overall feel of the title. A slow, delicate change of letters moving toward or away from each other is interesting and subtly dramatic, whereas rapid tracking changes with letters snapping toward or away from each other feels more energetic and action packed.

Check Text Alignment Before Tracking

Professional editing or graphics software, such as Final Cut Pro and LiveType, automatically align standard text objects to the center. Other applications such as Motion automatically align text to the left. The tracking controls move the text relative to the alignment of the text. Text with a center alignment will track the letters toward or away from the center of the text. Text with a left alignment will track letters toward or away from the left, and a right alignment will track letters toward or away from the right. Before you animate tracking, be sure to set the alignment of your text to match the direction from which you want the text to move.

Title Tracking Animation Techniques and Variations

Tracking animation can be used as a transition to make letters move together to form words or spread apart to remove words from the screen. It can also be used to make words breathe and seem alive without moving the actual text.

Each technique can be created at different speeds ranging from slow to rapid. Feel free to vary the duration and extent of the tracking changes to better fit your projects.

You'll find full-resolution still images or QuickTime movies on the companion DVD included with this book. The path is TITLE_DESIGN_ESSENTIALS > Chapter 4 > Tracking.

Title Tracking Animation Checklist

Before you add tracking animation to your text, consider these points.

✔ Do you want the text to appear or disappear with letters coming together or flying apart?

✔ What is the overall tone or feel of the project? Consider quick and drastic tracking changes for more energetic titles or slow and subtle tracking changes for more conservative titles.

✔ Do you want the letters in the text to move toward or away from each other?

✔ Do you want the letters to track toward the left, center, or right?

✔ Do you want the tracking change to lead to the final tracking value or away from the final tracking value?

✔ How long do you want to hold the text onscreen without changing the tracking?

✔ Do you want a continuous tracking change while the text is onscreen?

NOTE: If you've never modified text tracking before, take a moment to familiarize yourself with that feature before moving on to the title tracking animation techniques. Some software such as Motion or LiveType include prebuilt tracking effects. You can also animate tracking manually by adding keyframes to set the tracking value changes over time.

090 – ATTRACTION

The attraction technique moves the letters together to the final tracking value. This is often used in commercials, main titles, and credits to add movement to the text without actually changing the text's position. In most editing and motion graphics software the tracking follows the text alignment. In this example, the text was aligned left, so the letters move toward the first letter to reach the final position.

Tracking values for the attraction technique range from 3–5 to 0.

In this example, the tracking is animated from 3 to 0 and is left aligned.

Attraction	Attraction	Attraction	Attraction
Tracking 3	*Tracking 2*	*Tracking 1*	*Tracking 0*

This effect is often combined with fades and flying in or shrinking animation.

091 – REPELLING

Repelling is the opposite of the attraction animation and causes the text to spread apart. This technique is often seen in commercials and movie trailers.

Tracking values for the repelling technique start at 0 and increase to 3–5.

In this example, the tracking is animated from 0 to 3 and is left aligned.

Repelling	Repelling	Repelling	Repelling
Tracking 0	*Tracking 1*	*Tracking 2*	*Tracking 3*

This effect is often combined with fades and zooming out or growing animation.

Title Tracking Animation Techniques and Variations

092 – REVERSE SNAP IN/OUT

If the text is aligned left, you can use negative tracking values to move the text before the first letter and then snap it into position. This effect is fun for main titles and credits, especially for fast-paced or energetic projects. Negative tracking values move the letters to the left until they appear before the first letter; a tracking value of zero is the normal text character spacing.

Animate tracking from −100 to 0 to reverse snap the text in.

Animate tracking from 0 to −100 to reverse snap the text out.

Tracking −100   *Tracking −50*

Tracking −22   *Tracking −15*

Tracking −10   *Tracking 0*

This effect works well with a fast or swift fade in at the beginning of a reverse snap in and a fast or swift fade out at the end of a reverse snap out.

NOTE: Some applications will stack all of the letters instead of moving them off-screen to the left.

093 – TRACK OUT TRANSITION

Instead of a simple fade out, a more interesting transition is to track out the text so that the letters spread so far apart that they exit the frame. This technique adds great energy or action to the text. The effect can be timed to music or other action on the screen. A track out transition is commonly used in commercials and main titles.

Tracking 0   *Tracking 25*   *Tracking 100*   *Tracking 500*

This effect works even better when combined with a fade out at the end of the title.

094 – TRACK IN TRANSITION

Track in transition is the companion effect to the track out transition and produces an exciting entrance for titles. This technique is ideal for main titles of energetic projects or for adding action to an otherwise boring title sequence. Experiment with the duration to see the variations of the effect. A fast track in makes the letters look like they rush in and stand at attention, whereas a slow track in makes the letters look like they take their time and eventually gather to reveal the final text.

Tracking 500   Tracking 100   Tracking 25   Tracking 0

This effect works well with a fade in at the beginning of the title.

Position Animation

Text that moves from one position to another on the screen is a simple yet powerful form of title animation. Like other forms of title animation, the speed and extent of the changes in position greatly affect the overall look and feel of the text movement. Position animation allows text to enter, exit, start, stop, fly, creep, run, float, or bounce. Moving text also includes crawling text, which moves continually across the bottom or top of the screen, and scrolling text, which is used for credits at the end of a project.

Position changes are often used with main titles, credits, lower thirds, and interjections. Moving text is one of the most powerful forms of title animation because moving text will always be more compelling than static text.

There are four considerations when animating position:

- Where you want the text to start
- Where you want the text to end
- How fast you want the text to move
- The length of time you want the text onscreen

TITLE POSITION ANIMATION TECHNIQUES AND VARIATIONS

Animating position can be used as a transition to make text appear or disappear, to add a sense of visual movement toward or away from the screen, or simply to make the text seem more active. Here are some standard scale animation techniques that are commonly used with main titles, credits, and interjections.

Each technique can be created at different speeds ranging from extremely slow to ultra fast. Feel free to vary the speed and extent of the position changes to better fit your projects.

You'll find full-resolution still images or QuickTime movies on the companion DVD included with this book. The path is TITLE_DESIGN_ESSENTIALS > Chapter 4 > Position.

Title Position Animation Checklist

Before you add position animation to your text, consider these points.

✔ Do you want the text to enter or exit the frame?

✔ What is the overall tone or feel of the project? Consider fast text movement for more energetic titles or slow movement for more conservative titles.

✔ Where do you want the text to start, and where do you want the text to end?

✔ Do you want continuous text movement onscreen, or would you prefer that the text starts and stops?

✔ How long do you want the text to be onscreen?

NOTE: If you've never modified text position before, take a moment to familiarize yourself with that feature before moving on to the title position animation techniques. Some editing software includes prebuilt crawling, scrolling, pushing, and general movement transitions and effects. You can also animate position manually by adding keyframes to set the position value changes over time.

TITLE POSITION ANIMATION SETUP (APPLY TO PREPARED BASIC TITLES)

Requirements

Software
  Any nonlinear editing or motion graphics software with title generator

Recommended Layout Features
  Text position controls

Software Titling Advanced Features
  Keyframe or animation controls to change position values over time
  Optional: prebuilt position or moving text transitions

Time: 1–5 minutes

Preparation: Open a project containing a basic title. Select the text object and turn on or apply changes to the text position as needed.

095 – CRAWLING TEXT

Crawling text is used for emergency messages, stock reports, or news and can be located at the top or bottom of the screen. The most common location for crawling text is at the bottom of the screen just on or above the title safe boundary. Crawling text can move from right to left or left to right; the standard for words and sentences is to move right to left. The exception is for cultures that read from right to left; in that case, the text enters from the left side of the frame and moves toward the right. Almost all crawling text uses sans serifed fonts and capitalized letters, and the text is usually white or pale yellow.

Professional editing and motion graphics software should include prebuilt crawling text generators and effects. If not, create a very long title containing the text and animate the starting and ending position for a slow movement right to left across the bottom or top of the screen (within the title safe boundaries).

Make sure that the speed is slow enough that the text can be read, but fast enough to keep the audience's interest in reading the text. If the text moves too fast, the reader may get frustrated and give up.

Text on the title safe line

096 – SCROLLING TEXT

Scrolling text is generally used at the end of projects to display the end credits. It moves the text upward so that the text enters the screen at the bottom and exits at the top. Scrolling text is centered if it's a single column of information. If there are two columns of information, the left column is right justified, the right column is left justified, and there's a gap in the middle. As with crawling text, the scrolling text should move slowly enough for most people to read, yet fast enough so it doesn't drag on too long.

Many professional editing applications include prebuilt scrolling text generators and effects.

097 – ENTER/EXIT

The enter/exit technique for text movement gets its name from text that enters and/or exits the screen. Not only is it an interesting way for text to arrive and leave, it's also very easy to create. Simply set position values at the starting position and ending position. If the text will pause, add hold position coordinates to your animation keyframes. This type of movement can be in any direction and either move continuously or enter screen, pause, and then exit.

Enter/exit text is often used in commercials for interjections and key information, as well as main titles and credits.

098 – PUSH IN

Pushes are a great way for text to push on or off the screen. You can either use prebuilt push transitions or animate the push manually by setting the starting and ending positions.

A push in moves either right or left to push the text onscreen and into position.

Pushes are most commonly used for lower thirds and key information text.

099 – PUSH OUT

Push outs are the perfect exit strategy for lower thirds text. Generally, if text is pushed in from the right, it is then pushed out toward the left. Push outs are also used with key information text that enters using a push in effect.

100 – PUSH UP

Pushing text up into the frame is used less frequently but works great for slipping in key information and disclaimers that are near the bottom of the screen.

101 – PUSH DOWN

Pushing text down to move it offscreen is a common way to remove key information text, blurbs, and disclaimers that are already near the bottom of the screen.

102 – MOTION PATH

Motion paths can be prebuilt animation effects that you modify or can be created manually by setting position coordinates at different positions over time. The process for animating a motion path differs from application to application but should be possible in any professional editing or motion graphics program.

Motion paths are common for main titles, interjections, and credits that need to move in more than one direction.

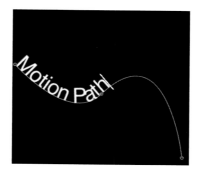

Motion path displayed

Text moving along the motion path

103 – CIRCLE PATH

Circle paths are great for text that needs to move in a circular pattern and can be modified so that the text moves on either the inside or outside of the path.

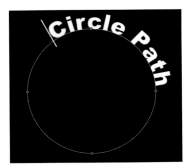

Circle path displayed (outside circle text)

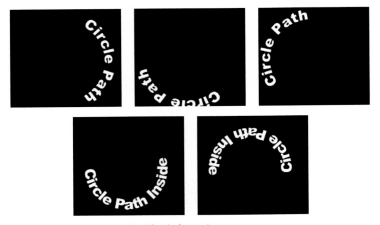

Circle path (inside circle text)

CHAPTER 5

Choreographing a Title Sequence

Choreography is the planning and execution of an event, and often refers to the movement of people or objects to music. Choreographing a title sequence is the careful planning and execution of titles to audio, video, or by title priority. If the project includes prominent sound effects, musical cues, or dialog you may want to choreograph the titles to the audio. Does the background video include large moving objects, people or things entering and exiting the frame or interesting transitions? If so you may wish to choreograph your titles based on the video. Perhaps the content of the titles is more important than anything else. If your key information titles, or other blurbs are crucial to a project's success, chances are the titles will be choreographed by title priority. In this chapter you'll get a taste of some of the most common and useful timing techniques for choreographing titles.

CHOREOGRAPHING TITLES TO AUDIO

TITLE CHOREOGRAPHY TO AUDIO SETUP (APPLY TO PREPARED TITLES)

Requirements

Software
Any nonlinear editing or motion graphics software with title generator

Recommended Layout Features
Grids, guides, or rulers for precision title alignment (optional)

Software Titling Advanced Features
Title Safe zones for title alignment

Time: 5–55 minutes depending on the number of titles and duration of title sequence

Preparation: Watch background video for title sequence. Listen to the audio and set markers in the timeline ruler for the prominent sound cues. Add titles at the sound cue points and animate accordingly. Modify animation, title position, and duration as needed.

Choreographing titles to audio means that the timing of the titles and their animation is based on audio cues. There are four different types of audio that can be used for timing titles including; music, vocal cues, sound effects, and literal animation to sound. If audio is a dominant element in a project, you may consider choreographing the titles to the audio.

Titles to Audio Checklist

Before you begin choreographing titles to audio, consider these points.

✔ What type of project is it?

✔ How important are the titles to the overall project? Are some of the titles more important than others and need special emphasis? If so, consider choreographing them to the audio for added emphasis.

✔ What is the overall tone of the project? If it is serious and conservative, you may want to use voice cues for the titles. If the project is fast paced or comical, literal audio cues and sound effect triggers can be a fun way to introduce titles.

✔ Is the audio that accompanies the titles primarily dialog, voice-over, or narration? If so, consider using the voice for title cues, especially if the text is repeating or paraphrasing the spoken words.

✔ Is the audio that accompanies the titles primarily music? Does the music have strong changes, beats, or instrumental parts that could be used to choreograph the titles?

✔ Are there dominant sound effects that could be used to trigger titles, such as a car crashing sound to cue a main title or a phone ringing to trigger a phone number?

✔ Could one or more of the titles mimic a sound effect or musical cue to animate literally, such as a jackhammer vibration, cymbal crashing, or rippling water?

✔ Are there strict time limits to the title sequence that would override creative choreography to audio?

NOTE: If you've never set markers for audio cues in the timeline, take a moment to familiarize yourself with that feature before moving on to the title choreography to audio techniques.

104 – TIME TO THE MUSIC

You don't have to be a musician to follow the beat or the rhythm of the music. Listen for dramatic changes in the music. Take advantage of those musical changes to introduce or remove titles. If the music is upbeat and active, try adding animation such as pushes, moves, or zooms that fit the pacing of the music. If the music is slow and easygoing, try transitions like fades. Throw in a little tracking or scale animation to accentuate musical highlights like cymbal swells or wind chimes.

105 – FOLLOW THE VOCAL CUES

If the project has voice-over that reads the same text as the titles shown, try to display the text a little bit ahead of the voice-over. Fade out the old text before the voice gets to the end and have subsequent text fade up before the voice gets to it. That way the reader can follow along, but the voice-over never gets ahead of the titles.

If the project is a documentary or news story where someone is introduced, you can hold back the lower third text until the person is introduced and then bring in the lower third text to reinforce the introduction. You can also do the opposite and slide in the lower third text to introduce the person right before he or she is announced vocally. Showing the person's name in print before it is spoken is advantageous because the audience can read the name as it is spoken, which makes the name more memorable. Both techniques are effective, and you can experiment with the timing as needed. Be aware that if you animate the lower third text while the name is being announced, the audience may be distracted by the animation and miss the introduction altogether.

For list text, if the list is also read aloud, you can introduce the new item in the list as it is spoken, just before it is spoken, or just after. Keep in mind that if the title comes before the dialog, you steal the thunder (idea) from the spokesperson. If the title text comes at the same time, the titles feel in sync with the spokesperson—like a cohesive team or an extension of the spokesperson. If the titles come in late, after they are spoken, they feel like a recap or sidekick to the announcer. Whichever look you prefer, be consistent with all of the titles in the list.

106 – SOUND EFFECT TRIGGERS

Some projects have sound effects, such as waves crashing, thunder, or race cars passing, during the title sequence. Try animating the titles to the sound effects if they are prominent. In this example the sound of the phone ringing triggers the phone number to appear onscreen.

107 – LITERAL ANIMATION TO SOUND

If the project is light hearted, comedic, or fun, you can animate the titles to imitate a sound effect or musical transition. For example, a title could shake erratically to the sound of an alarm clock. Programs such as Apple's LiveType and Motion include prebuilt title animation that you can apply to your text for more literal animation.

CHOREOGRAPHING TITLES TO VIDEO

Choreographing titles to video means the timing of the titles and their animation is based on the action, movement, or timing of the background video.

Titles to Video Checklist

Before you begin choreographing titles to video, consider these points.

✔ What type of project is it?

✔ How important are the titles to the overall project? Are some of the titles more important than others and need special emphasis? If so, consider keeping choreographing them to the video for added emphasis.

✔ What is the overall tone of the project? If it is serious and conservative, you may want to stick with classic fades for title animation; however, you can still time the titles based on the cuts or action in the video.

✔ Is the project fast-paced and exciting? If so, you could choreograph some of the titles to follow the cutting (editing) rhythm of the video, such as quick titles for quick shots and longer titles for longer shots.

✔ Does the video editing include transitions between shots that could also be applied to the title, such as a page peel, push, or wipe?

✔ Does the video include large moving elements with action that the titles could match?

✔ Do characters or objects enter or exit the frame? If so, the titles may be able to enter and/or exit at the same time.

✔ Do characters or objects move in a specific direction that the titles may follow, match, or pass going in the opposite direction?

✔ Is there some kind of action occurring onscreen that the titles could literally mimic, such as pouring, spinning, rotating, or spilling?

✔ Are there strict time limits to the title sequence that would override creative choreography to video?

TITLE CHOREOGRAPHY TO VIDEO SETUP (APPLY TO PREPARED TITLES)

Requirements
Software
 Any nonlinear editing or motion graphics software with title generator

Recommended Layout Features
 Grids, guides, or rulers for precision title alignment (optional)

Software Titling Advanced Features
 Title Safe zones for title alignment

Time: 5–55 minutes depending on the number of titles and duration of title sequence

Preparation: Watch background video for title sequence. Look for video elements that can be used to cue titles and set markers in the timeline ruler. Add titles at the video cue points and animate accordingly. Modify animation, title position, and duration as needed.

NOTE: If you've never set markers in the timeline, take a moment to familiarize your-self with that feature before moving on to the title choreography to video techniques.

108 – CUT TO CUT

The cut to cut technique uses titles that match the length of the video clips so that cutting to a new shot also cuts to a new title. There are no transitions for these titles; they simply exist as if they are part of a shot. With each new shot, a new title appears. This technique can be very effective for fast-paced pieces that warrant quick titles. You can also include titles on every other shot for more staggered cut style titles.

109 – MATCH ACTION

Another interesting and more eye-catching technique is to match the action of the title to an object or person moving onscreen. The title doesn't have to be over the object, it just has to match the movement. This can be fun for movements like a taxi cab driving across the screen or a dog walking, pausing, and then continuing off the screen.

110 – OPPOSITE DIRECTION

A variation of the match action is to use the opposite action. If the object is moving right to left, try moving the title left to right so that the object and the title pass each other in the middle. This works well for shots of airplanes, race cars, or other fast-moving objects.

111 – VIDEO TRANSITIONS

Transitions titling works similarly to the cut to cut technique except there's a transition on both the video and titles over the shots so that the video and the titles are affected alike. This technique can be used to reveal one title beneath the other in the same way the video is revealed, such as the edge wipe in the first example. You can also use a transition like a push so that the title follows the image, as shown in the second example.

112 – CHARACTER ENTRANCE AND EXIT

When an actor or character appears onscreen for the first time, it's sometimes nice to have a title (perhaps his or her credit) appear at the same time. And when the character exits the frame, you can use that action as a cue to have the title exit as well. However, this entrance and exit technique only works if the character is onscreen for a short time—five or six seconds. Otherwise, you can pick either the character's entrance or exit to cue the title.

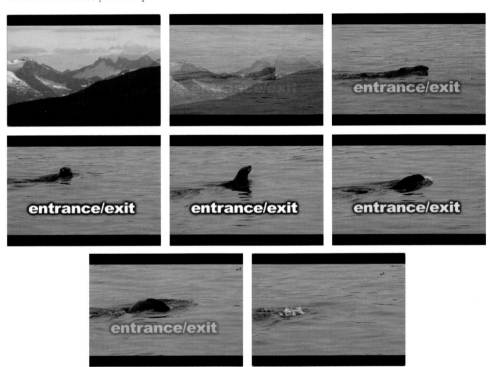

113 – LITERAL ANIMATION TO VIDEO

The literal animation to video technique animates the title to mimic the action of the video. In the example, the title pours onscreen over a shot of transmission fluid that is being poured into a torque converter.

NOTE: If you work on projects that could use a lot of literal-type title animation, you could animate them yourself or check out LiveType or Motion. Both applications include dozens of prebuilt title animations.

114 – GO WITH THE FLOW

If you plan to add a main title at the very beginning of a piece, go with the flow of the introduction. This is most common with television shows that have a limited amount of time to get through the initial title sequence. Start the title transitions when the video fades up. If you have a two-part title, bring in one title element at a time to stagger the text and build the title as the images build. If the images are big, bright, and flashy, the titles can follow suit. Use the flow of the project, movement, sound, and visuals to cue the timing of your titles.

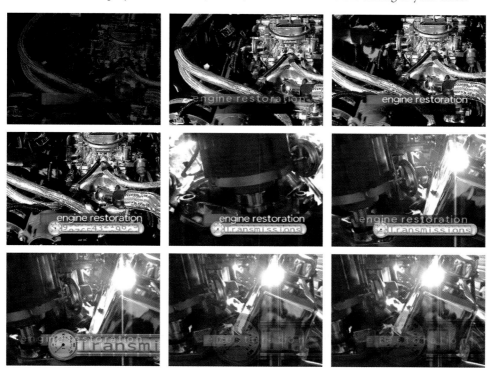

NOTE: The previous example includes two LiveFonts, which are available in LiveType and Motion. Remember that title design is all about choosing the right font, style, color, layout, and animation for a project. Once you understand all of those principles, you can experiment with more advanced titling tools like LiveFonts. These are fully animated fonts that do everything from shimmer, flame, walk, and sparkle.

CHOREOGRAPHING BY TITLE PRIORITY

CHOREOGRAPHY BY TITLE PRIORITY SETUP (APPLY TO PREPARED TITLES)

Requirements
Software
Any nonlinear editing or motion graphics software with title generator

Recommended Layout Features
Grids, guides, or rulers for precision title alignment (optional)

Software Titling Advanced Features
Title Safe zones for title alignment

Time: 5–55 minutes depending on the number of titles and duration of title sequence

Preparation: Calculate the duration for each title based on the length of the title sequence and the number of titles. Determine the minimum duration needed for each title. Allocate more time to titles of greater priority, and less time (minimums) to titles with the lowest priority. If there isn't enough time for each title to appear separately onscreen, pair up the lower priority titles, or build the key information like a business card.

Choreographing titles by title priority means that the timing of the titles is based on the importance of the content, contractual obligations, or how long a title needs to be onscreen. Three title priorities override all other titling considerations.

Choreography by Title Priority Checklist

Before you begin choreographing by title priority, consider these points.

✔ What type of project is it?

✔ How important are the titles to the overall project? Are some of the titles more important than others and need special emphasis? If so, consider keeping them onscreen longer than other lower-priority titles.

✔ What time constraints if any are there for the title sequence? If there is a limited amount of time, calculate how many titles you need to show and what is the minimum amount of time they can be onscreen. If there is time remaining after each title is onscreen for the minimum amount of time, extend the duration of the more important titles based on their priority.

✔ Are there strict time limits to the title sequence that would override creative choreography to video or audio?

✔ Does the project have exciting music, sound effects, or visuals? You may be tempted to edit the titles based on those factors; however, if you need to choreograph the titles based on the priority of the content or contractual agreement, focus on your goal. You can consider the overall layout for title placement, but the timing should be based only on the titles.

✔ Do you have a lot of titles to squeeze into a short amount of time? Try placing more than one onscreen at a time with faster dissolves and transitions.

✔ Are some or all of the titles necessary to fulfill a contractual or legal obligation? If so, make sure that they adhere to the minimums required.

TIP: It's a good idea to double-check all key information text, intellectual property rights titles, disclaimers, and text blocks before choreographing the final title sequence. Have someone from the legal department or the producer sign off on the content of the titles.

115 – TITLES VERSUS TIME

Time can be a real issue for commercials, public service announcements, and even credit sequences for television because there is a finite amount of viewing time. For example, a 30 second commercial has to include the entire commercial and the text. If a commercial includes key information, interjections, block text, and disclaimers, there isn't much time for each of the titles to be onscreen. Once again, it is usually key information text that needs the most screen time so viewers have time to actually read the text. You may want to fade titles up individually for maximum impact. However, if you have many titles and little onscreen time, you could use short transitions or place all the titles onscreen at the same time like a business card. Once they all fit, you can fade some elements in or out as needed but leave the more important titles up longer.

116 – CONTRACTUAL OBLIGATIONS

If an actor's or director's contract states that his or her title needs to be the same size and the same timing as the main title, then that's that. There is no flexibility on the timing. Once you set the timing of the main title, all the contingent titles will be timed accordingly. You may be able to use one of the audio or video techniques to dictate when you start or end the title, but the length must be the predetermined length. Be sure to check all contractual obligations before you start building a title sequence with a main title and credits.

117 – CONTENT

The content of the title may override visual aesthetics or creative timing. This is most common with key information text because working with this type of text isn't about entertainment, it's about making sure viewers can see the information and have time to read it. You hope they remember it, but that's out of your hands. A 30 second commercial might display the phone number for the company on the screen for the entire commercial, whereas other text may come and go as needed.

CHAPTER 6

Creating Project-based Titles

Now that you've learned about the different types of titles and adding drop shadows, outlines, color, gradients, basic animation, and choreography, it's time to put it all together to design real-world titles for four different types of projects. You'll start with the lower third titles for a documentary. Then you'll move on to a training video that needs list text. Next, you'll add text blocks and key information text to a Public Service Announcement, and finally you'll create the main title, credits, and intellectual property rights for a video podcast. For each title scenario you'll evaluate the background, choose a font, modify the size and style of the text, and then add a drop shadow, outlines, and animation as needed. But first, it's a good idea to take a few minutes to understand the different types of backgrounds that you may encounter in your titling work and how the backgrounds affect title design and layout.

Evaluating the Background

Many factors can affect your title design. The necessity for titles means that one way or another the titles must be created and fit on the screen. When, where, and how is up to you. One of the most powerful elements in title design is the background. Backgrounds can either limit or stimulate your creativity depending on the situation. Your best course of action is to arm yourself with information so that you can quickly access the backgrounds in your projects and design titles accordingly.

Two primary considerations when looking at the background are content and composition. The content includes the format of the background and the focus or movement. Composition refers to the texture, layout, and color.

Let's look at examples of the different content and composition elements, and see how they influence title design.

NOTE: If you have a design background, you may already know many of these design principles; however, you may not understand how they affect title design. If you are new to design principles, this section will not only open your eyes to these elements, but like any new skill, you'll also probably become acutely aware of them as you watch television, movies, or videos in your daily life. As you train your eye for composition details, you won't be able to watch television the same again (for a while anyway). Not only that, but you may even want to share these ideas with friends and family.

Identifying the Background Content

When evaluating the background for your titles, you first need to identify the content. The content of the background includes the format and focus or movement of the scene.

Here are some examples of the different types of background content.

SOLID COLOR

Solid color formats can be any solid color, black, or white. These are the easiest backgrounds to work with because they offer no visual competition for the text. On the other hand, they aren't very stimulating and don't add anything to the titles either. The only limitation with solid colored backgrounds is that you can't use the same color for your text without adding a drop shadow or outline to separate it from the background. Many different colors will look great over the solid. If the background is a dark color, try using white or a light color for your text. If the background is light colored, try using black or a darker hue of the same color. You could also use the opposite color on the color wheel. If the title warrants extra attention, try a color gradient in the text.

GRADIENT

Gradient backgrounds include a blending of several colors in a vertical, horizontal, diagonal, or radial direction. Gradient backgrounds are very text friendly. The only visual competition is where the colors meet; other than that it's a wide open canvas for your text. Gradient backgrounds don't require drop shadows or outlines to see the text. However, you may add drop shadows or outlines to stylize the text a little. If so, consider using one of the gradient colors in the text, outline, or drop shadow. Another interesting alternative is to use the opposite colors for the text, drop shadow, or outline.

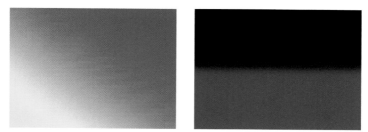

PATTERN/TEXTURE

Patterns and textured backgrounds can be much more visually stimulating, and potentially compete with the text. Most patterns and textures, like the examples here from LiveType, use subdued pastel colors or various shades of the same color. It is easy to see solid text over pastel colors and shades of the same color. Try using one of the background colors in the text, outline, or drop shadow to dress up the titles and make the background and titles feel coordinated instead of like two separate items.

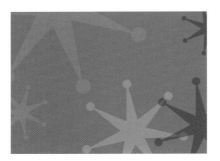

COMPUTER-GENERATED IMAGERY (CGI)

Computer-generated imagery (CGI), like these examples from LiveType, can be a simple graphic, subtle pattern, or complex animated scene. If the background looks like a pattern or texture, treat it as such. If there is complex action on the screen, you'll treat it as you would motion picture or video footage. These CGI examples are fairly busy and may require a drop shadow, outline, or solid object to separate the text from the background.

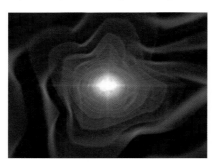

MOTION PICTURE/VIDEO

Motion pictures and video footage can contain virtually anything as the subject matter. When working with motion picture or video footage, it is important that you study the footage carefully and base your titling choices on the overall composition. The font may be influenced by a project's subject matter, but the title design layout will likely be contingent on the composition of the images, not the thematic content. You'll learn more about composition shortly.

STILL IMAGES

Still images include photographs and graphics. The subject matter can vary as much as motion picture footage, but the difference is that the still images don't contain any movement. The good news is that it's easier to evaluate the composition of an image that doesn't change, so it speeds up the title design process. The downside is that the image doesn't move so it may not be as visually stimulating. You can always add a little movement by animating the titles.

Identifying the Background Focus or Movement

The focus or movement of the background is one the most important considerations when designing your title layout. Focus, in this case, refers to the point of interest, or subject of the image. Movement indicates whether there is actual movement of the camera or within the frame. There are a lot of different compositional elements to consider, but chances are the focus or movement will suggest, inspire, or demand where your titles will be placed.

What's the big deal about focus and movement? If there is something interesting happening onscreen, you don't want to cover it up with titles. If the camera is moving, you need to know the whole shot from start to finish to lay out the titles and make sure they don't cover up anything important.

STATIC

Static background images, as the name suggests, contain no movement. The camera doesn't move, and the subject doesn't move much either. Static images include stills, gradients, solid colors, graphics, textures, patterns, or motion picture/video footage that contains no tangible movement. In the following examples, the first static shot is of an engine. The engine may be running and perhaps there is a minor vibration, but for all intents and purposes there is no movement you would need to worry about covering up with your titles. The second example is a close-up shot of a flower. The flower doesn't move except for the occasional breeze, but unless it's a gale force wind that knocks the flower around in the frame, there is no tangible movement. Medium or close shots of people talking (also known as talking head shots) are considered static because the camera doesn't move and their heads barely move; the only things moving are their mouths and eyes, which you wouldn't cover up with text in the first place. Sometimes, the most interesting element onscreen *is* the titles. In that case, put them wherever you want, except over someone's face.

CAMERA MOVEMENT

A camera can move a lot or just a little during a shot. Here are some examples that illustrate the beginning, middle, and end of some standard camera moves. As you can see in each example, the beginning of the shot is quite different from the end. If a title needs to go over a moving camera shot, study the entire sequence first before determining where to place the titles.

Example of a pull out (zoom out) move

Example of a dolly in move

Example of a pan right

Example of a tilt up

MOVEMENT WITHIN THE FRAME

Another option to consider for title placement is movement within the frame while the camera remains static. Movement within the frame can be anything from a bolt of lightning to a stampeding herd of buffalo. Chances are, whatever is moving is important to the overall project, or simply the most interesting item on the screen. Just be aware of it, and try not to cover it up. The exception would be if the moving subject fills the entire screen. In that case you have no choice but to cover up some of it.

These examples show varying degrees of movement within the frame. The shot of the bay is relatively static but contains three moving elements: the water, the sailboat, and a seagull in the upper-right corner of the frame. The water is barely moving so it's a nonissue. The seagull is really small, and unless this is a project about seagulls, it won't get much attention. The sailboat, on the other hand, is interesting and sure to draw attention. Fortunately, there is plenty of room above and below the sailboat to add titles without covering it up.

The second example is a static shot in the woods with a stream running through it. In this case, the stream is the only movement. Once again, unless the stream is the subject of the entire project, you don't have to worry about covering up part of it with titles as needed.

The third example includes a honeybee bustling about the flower. The bee is more interesting than anything else, so it would be nice to place the titles in the upper left where the background is out of focus and the bee can continue about his business anywhere on the flower.

The fourth example is a close shot of someone grinding and shaping engine parts. The hand moves the part around and sparks rain downward. In this situation the part and sparks are interesting, and important to the show, so any titles would need to go in the upper third or left side of the frame.

AREA OF INTEREST/POINT OF FOCUS

With or without movement, another consideration is an area of interest or point of focus within the frame. If you can identify the most interesting part of an image, you can avoid covering it up with titles. Each of the following examples has a clear point of interest where the audience will be focusing its attention.

The points of focus in these examples are obvious: chipmunk, royal guard, fireman and/or flames, and statue.

Identifying the Background Composition

Once you've identified the focus or movement of the background, you can look at the composition to help you plan and refine your title design. Three composition factors can inspire or limit your design choices: canvas, layout, and color. Let's start with the canvas.

Understanding the Canvas Composition

As a title design artist, you need to assess your canvas before you start applying text. Backgrounds can offer a variety of canvas types and textures from smooth and clean to busy and chaotic. Here are a few examples and how they might affect your titles.

SMOOTH AND CLEAN

A smooth and clean canvas (background) has plenty of open space for applying text. Solid colored backgrounds are as smooth and clean as it gets, but some color, mild gradient, or even an object or two are okay as long as they don't impede your title placement. A smooth and clean background fits two primary criteria: you can place text virtually anywhere you want, and plain text (without shadow or outline) will work. This doesn't mean that you can't style the text with outlines or shadows. It simply means that you don't have to in order to see the text against the background.

TEXTURED OR DIRTY

If the background image contains complex objects that take up most of the screen or textured patterns, it could be considered textured or dirty. Dirty in the sense that there isn't a large frame of clean space to apply text, not actual dirt on the background. Text can still be applied to textured or dirty backgrounds; you just may need to add a drop shadow or outline to help the text stand out.

Each of these examples offers a different textured or dirty canvas challenge. The flower is fairly smooth, but the fact that the color changes would make white or light text difficult to see.

The engine shot presents a text challenge because of the dramatic difference between the light and dark sections. The light section on the left side isn't quite large enough for much text, and the dark areas have engine parts in the way. Text over this background will need an outline, drop shadow, or both to help it stand out. The other option is to try brightly colored text, which would stand out over the chunks of dark background.

The two textured patterns are from LiveType and are actually moving backgrounds. The lines of the blue weave pattern jiggle, and the pastel pattern is moving as well. In either case you could try plain text, but it would be hard to see against the background unless the text is very large. An opposite color such as yellow or orange might work over either texture. Another option is light text with a dark outline or drop shadow, or dark text with a light outline or drop shadow.

BUSY OR CHAOTIC

Busy or chaotic backgrounds have so much going on visually that plain text or text with a simple shadow or outline is almost impossible to read. When you're dealing with a really busy or chaotic background, you will likely have to place your text on a solid shape of some kind. The top two examples are static images, but they are so busy that there's no place to put the text so it would be clearly seen. The lower LiveType backgrounds are both very chaotic and show constant movement in different directions. Once again, the solution is to add a solid or blurred shape to use as a life raft for the text.

MIXED

Mixed canvas backgrounds are a combination of smooth, busy, and/or textured elements. The exact smooth to textured or busy ratio doesn't matter as long as there are some clean or smooth places to add text within the frame. Generally, grass and sky are fairly reliable sources of clean space for text.

Defining the Background Layout

The composition principles for title design layout that were illustrated in Chapter 1, "Creating Effective Basic Titles," also apply to the background layout. Let's take a look at examples of each type of background layout, starting with rhythm.

RHYTHM

If the background follows a rhythmic or musical type pattern, it is likely a rhythm layout. Each of these examples differs but has its own rhythm. The hypnotic blue circles in the first image have a definite rhythm. The black dots in the second example follow a sweeping rhythmic pattern. The third example may be a little harder to define, but the red flowers form a nice pattern. If you look carefully, the pairs of red flowers flow across the frame like chords in musical notation. When the background has a distinctive rhythm layout, it's a good idea to use a similar layout for your titles to continue or enhance the overall rhythm of the scene.

 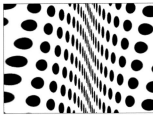 

SYMMETRICAL

A symmetrical layout is planned and aligns elements carefully to the center of the frame or to each other. Usually, symmetrical backgrounds are very balanced. Cut the image down the middle and you have two equal halves. Symmetrical layouts are often centered or follow a vertical, horizontal, diagonal, or circular layout. The best title design strategy for a symmetrical layout is to follow the same symmetry with your titles to balance rather than upset the overall look and feel of the piece.

ASYMMETRICAL

Asymmetrical composition is more free flowing and interesting. You can often identify an asymmetrical background by the fact that there is no distinct horizontal, vertical, centered, or diagonal alignment theme. Asymmetrical backgrounds usually offer a variety of text placement options because you don't have to worry about upsetting a symmetrical or rhythmic background. Respect the asymmetric flow and place your text where it *feels* right rather than measuring coordinates or aligning to a specific object.

SPACE

Space layout usually involves one or two prominent objects arranged in an interesting way within the frame. When you first glance at an image using space composition, you often see the empty or negative space as prominently as the subject. When adding text to a space composition, respect the space when you determine whether it's best to place text over the subject or in the negative space. Sometimes the negative space is better left alone.

THIRDS

One of the most common background compositions is the use of thirds. You can recognize a background that uses the rule of thirds because the prominent elements in the image are framed to fit in the horizontal, or vertical, thirds of the frame. A thirds composition is visually balanced with two thirds containing subjects of lesser significance and one third framing the primary subject. In a thirds composition either one or two thirds can be left empty. Sometimes you can clearly see how the image falls into thirds, such as a landscape with land in the lower third, water in the middle, and sky in the upper third. Other times the subject or subjects may be in vertical thirds. Whether the image is composed in thirds horizontally, vertically, or both, try to use the principle for placing text.

Can you see how the rule of thirds applies to the following examples? Keep in mind that leaving one or two thirds empty is still following the rule.

Horizontal thirds

Vertical thirds

Identifying the Background Color

The last thing that you need to consider when building your titles is the background color. Identifying the primary background colors as well the dominant or highlight colors can help you determine what color, if any, to add to the text. When discussing color for titles, the color or colors could be applied to the text, shadow, or outline.

BLACK AND WHITE (GRAYSCALE)

Black and white (grayscale) backgrounds could be solid black, solid white, solid gray, or any combination from texture, to pattern, to a photograph. You can follow two color strategies when working with black and white (grayscale) backgrounds: keep the text grayscale to match or add a splash of color. You first need to determine *why* the image is black and white. Is the project a period piece and black and white for a reason? Is it black and white to deemphasize the background? Is it black and white for stylistic reasons? Is it black and white so the titles will be the only color and therefore really stand out in the overall title sequence? Solid black or white titles with an outline or shadow of the opposite color look great over black and white images. You could also use gray text with a black or white outline and shadows. The more dramatic the background, the more dramatic the outline and shadows can be. If you're adding color, remember that yellow or red demand the most attention. The good news is that any color you add, even if it is only the shadow or outline, will separate the text from the background and attract the viewer's eye.

MONOCHROMATIC/SHADES

Backgrounds that are monochromatic (one color) or shades offer many text color choices as well. You could use black or white, the same color as the image with a contrasting outline or shadow, or an opposite (complementary) color. In these examples the bay shot is a grayish blue, so the text could be black, white, gray, or some of the gray/blue from the image. Since the color is so muted in this example, almost any color would stand out against the background. Since the image is fairly plain, you could also jazz up the text a bit with a gradient that includes the darkest or lightest color in the image.

The second example is a dark yellow texture with shimmering, vibrating threads. Solid black or white text would work okay but the text would look even better with a contrasting shadow or outline to help separate it from the active background. If you want to color the text, you could use yellow text (any shade that matches the image) with a contrasting outline or shadow. You could also use the complementary purple color or any other bright color.

The same goes for the last example. Even though the background is moving, it is still pretty clean and smooth for applying text. Black and white text or text in a solid dark color that matches one in the image would stand out nicely. You could also color the text using the lightest hue from the image, but you'll need to add an outline or shadow to separate it from the light areas of the background.

  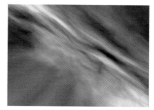

GRADIENTS/TEXTURES AND LIMITED COLORS

Gradients, textures, and other images with a limited number of colors (2–4) have a few limitations, but also offer great opportunities to add color to the text. All three of the examples include two or more colors to choose from for the text. Try selecting one of the colors from the image to use for the text and another for the drop shadow or outline. You could also use black or white text and accent it with a drop shadow or outline that includes a color from the image. Complementary colors are another option if the image is fairly textured or busy. Try using an opposite color from the background where the text will be, or use the complementary color as the drop shadow or outline. In the example with the diagonal gradient, you could use the darker color for the text if it is placed over the lighter colored section, or use the lighter color for the text if it is placed over the darker section. You can also use a color that matches the part of the gradient the text is on, but use the other gradient color to accessorize the text with an outline or shadow.

MULTICOLORED

If the background image is multicolored (more than four colors), your text will compete with the other colors in the image. You could try using a darker or lighter version of a color that is in the image, use a color that exactly matches one in the image, or for fun try using a color that isn't used in the image. If you try the last approach and choose a color that is not already in the background, choose a saturation of the color that fits in with the image. Saturation refers to how heavy a color is. Lightly saturated colors are pastels; heavily saturated colors are much deeper and darker. In the second multicolored example, the color of the man's shirt is a light to medium blue. You could try the same color to accent the text or choose a different color, like a light to medium yellow, for contrast. The idea is to match the feel of the background. If the background uses bright colors, the text should use bright colors too.

DOMINANT AND HIGHLIGHT COLORS

Sometimes images have a clearly dominant color that can be used to influence your text color. If one color stands out when you glance at an image, that color is dominant. Many images also have a highlight or detail color that complements the dominant one. Think of the image as a room. When you walk in the first thing you may notice is the overall color scheme, or lack thereof. That color scheme would be the dominant color of the room. You'll probably also notice the color of the trim or accents around the room if they are distinguishable from the dominant color. Both the dominant color and the highlight color of an image make great color choices for text. You can also mix and match them, using one for the text and the other for the outline or shadow.

Each of the top three examples has a clear dominant color when you glance at the image. The second color that you notice is the highlight or accent. In the first example the sky blue is the dominant color, and the yellow/gold color of Big Ben and the Parliament building is the highlight. In the second shot blue is once again the dominant color, and the yellow horizon is the highlight. The third example has a radiating textured background. Orange/red is the dominant color, and yellow or white could be the highlight depending on which you prefer.

Some images have obvious dominant colors and highlights, and others are harder to find for the untrained eye. Can you see the dominant or highlight colors in the last three examples?

The brownish gray of the engine shop is the dominant color, and the red or silver of the engine could be the highlight. The telephone booth red is the dominant color, and the gold from the crown or reflection could be the highlight. The dominant color in the flowers shot is less obvious. You could consider the green background dominant or the pastel pink of the flowers. The yellow center of the flowers would make a nice highlight or the pink from the petals if you choose green as the dominant color. Remember, not all images have a clear dominant or highlight color.

Training Your Inner Designer

Before you move on to the next section, take a moment to evaluate the images in the first part of this chapter. The more you practice evaluating image composition, the easier it becomes. As you look at each image, try to answer the following questions.

- What is the focus or movement of the image?

- What type of canvas is the background: smooth, textured, busy, or mixed?

- What is the design layout of the background?

- Does the image have a few colors or many? Is there a dominant color? Is there a highlight color?

- Where would you place text over the image, and what color would it be?

Casting Titles That Complement a Project

Casting titles is like casting the characters for a narrative project. Casting includes the personality of the text (font), wardrobe (color, shadow, or outline), and action (animation). Main titles are the lead characters that influence the entire piece. The other titles are supporting characters.

The time has come to put your titling skills to the text (pun intended). This section includes four different types of projects that need title casting (design) for specific titles. For each titling project, you are welcome to import the background movie from the companion DVD into your own software and follow along or simply read through the steps to follow my titling logic, and then try it on your own later and create your own design.

Keep in mind that title design is highly subjective, and there are as many design options and ideas as there are designers. These projects are designed to illustrate the title design workflow and offer suggestions that you can apply to your own projects in the future.

 You'll find the background movies (without text) for each example and finished QuickTime movies with titles on the companion DVD included with this book. The path is TITLE_DESIGN_ESSENTIALS > Chapter 6.

Title Casting Checklist

Before you start designing your titles for a project consider these points.

✔ What type of project is it?

✔ Is there a theme or overall feel?

✔ What type of title do you need to design?

✔ Where will this project be seen? big screen? portable screen? television? all screens?

✔ Identify the focus or movement of the background.

✔ Is the canvas clean or busy? Will you need to add backing elements like solids, lines, or shapes to go behind the text?

✔ What is the background layout/composition?

✔ What is the overall color scheme of the background?

✔ How much time do the titles need to be onscreen?

NOTE: The projects that you'll be working on are fictional; however, the titling techniques and process are the same as they would be if the projects were real.

DESIGN LOWER THIRD TEXT
FOR A DOCUMENTARY

For this project we'll come up with the overall design of the lower third text for a documentary. The same design can be used throughout the project with subtle variations as needed.

Let's first go through the title casting checklist.

✔ The project is a documentary on the past, present, and future of San Francisco bay area wildlife.

✔ The theme or feel is thoughtful, reflective, and overall positive.

✔ The titles to be designed are lower third text.

✔ This is a television documentary, so the titles need to be TV safe and large enough to read on television.

✔ The focus or movement of the background for the first title is a panning shot from left to right that shows the Golden Gate Bridge, and then a dissolve to a shot of the bay with Alcatraz, a sailboat, and the San Francisco-Oakland Bay Bridge in the background.

✔ The canvas is pretty clean with plenty of space to add titles, but we might consider an outline or drop shadow to add contrast to the monochromatic look of the scene. The right text style won't have any trouble being seen over the background.

✔ The background layout is thirds with content in the middle horizontal third. Titles could go nicely in the upper or lower third. Since the needed titles are lower thirds, that decision has already been made for us. However, in studying the background shot, most of the action, or points of interest, are on the left side of the frame. Since lower thirds can be anywhere on the lower third, let's place them on the lower right side of the frame leave.

✔ The color is a monochromatic gray/blue with plenty of shades to choose from to use in the text.

✔ The shots are long and slow to accommodate the narration, so the titles won't be rushed. They should be up long enough for a slow reader to read through.

CHOOSE A FONT AND TEST IT IN BLACK AND WHITE

The first step is to select a font and view it in both black and white to test the waters, literally and figuratively in this case. Checking a font in both black and white over the background helps you determine whether dark or light text will work better over the background. You can also take this time to size the text since it is lower third text.

It's a good idea to use easy to read boldface fonts for lower third text. For this project, let's use the sans serifed font Arial Black. This font works for almost any situation, is clean and easy to read, and has a contemporary feel.

Create two text objects: The first is San Francisco Bay and the second is 2010. You'll need to create two objects because later you'll animate them differently, and the date comes in after the other text. Make one object black text and the other white text.

Place the text objects in the lower third of the frame within the TV safe (title safe) zone. Play the background movie and see which is easier to read. If both the black and white text works well, you'll have more options for choosing a text color.

Although the black and white text stands out pretty well, the black is too strong for this subdued image, and the white is a bit too stark.

CHANGE THE BLACK TEXT TO A DARK COLOR FROM WITHIN THE BACKGROUND

Select a dark color from the background, such as the darkest blue/gray, to use instead of black for the darker text. Then change the white text to a light color from the image. How does the text look now?

If the dark- and light-colored text both look good (as they do in this example), you could try combining them using one color for the text and another for the outline or shadow, or try a gradient using both colors. In this scene a gradient might be too decorative. Since the lighter color shows up better against the water, we'll ultimately use that for the text and the darker color for the outline.

You may notice that the text looks a little lost there in the corner. The size is fine, but it could use some graphics.

ADD LOWER THIRD GRAPHICS

Lower thirds are usually embellished with either a subtle or fully animated graphic to frame the text. Since the shot and the overall project is thoughtful and reflective, it wouldn't be appropriate to add a full-blown lower third graphic with flashy lightning bolt patterns and sparkles as you might see on the morning news programs. Instead, let's consider the layout again. The background uses a thirds layout, but you'll also notice prominent horizontal lines. Let's add a dark and light line that will hold the text like a pier without dominating the frame.

You can create the lines in an application like Adobe Photoshop or create them in your editing or motion graphics software. In this case, the title was made in Final Cut Pro, so I added a colored matte and simply cropped it to the size and position I wanted for each colored line.

After you've created the lines, color one with the same dark color that you used for the dark text, and color the other line with a medium color from the background.

Place the San Francisco Bay title so that it sits on the dark line.

Then place the 2010 title so that it hangs from the lower line.

NOTE: Don't worry about the text colors at this point. Your goal right now is to finish the layout of the titles and graphic. You can finish coloring the text thereafter. It is important to complete the layout before coloring the text because the layout may affect which colors you use and how you use them. If you color the text first and then do the layout, you'll likely need to tweak the colors to fit the alignment to the lower third graphics.

The layout is complete.

REFINE THE COLORS AND STYLE TO FIT THE GRAPHICS

After you've finished the layout, you can refine the text colors. Since the light color stands out better against the background, let's use the light color for both pieces of text and the dark graphic color for the outline. For this project let's use a dramatic outline (041).

The outlined text really fits nicely with the lower third graphic and stands out well against the background without competing with the points of interest in the video.

ADD ANIMATION TO BRING THE TEXT IN AND OUT OF FRAME

When the composition and coloring of the text are finished, you can add some tasteful animation that fits with the piece. In this case, since it is a lower third title, let's add a push in from the right (098) to introduce the lines and a classic fade in (077) to introduce the San Francisco Bay part of the title. The date text doesn't appear until the shot changes.

A fast fade in (080) will work nicely to introduce the date once the sailboat shot is onscreen.

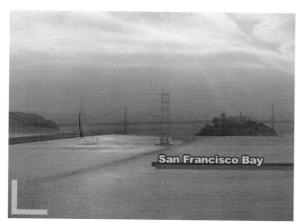

Once the text has finished its debut, it's time to plan its exit strategy. A push out from the left toward the right (099) will work well for the lines plus the San Francisco Bay text, and a fast fade out (080) will work well for the date.

That's it! Mission accomplished. You can now use the same lower third title as a template for other scenes in the show.

VARY THE LOWER THIRDS OCCASIONALLY TO KEEP YOUR AUDIENCE INTERESTED

For interest, try varying the outline or text colors slightly, such as in this example where the upper text is the same style as the template, but the lower text reverses the light and dark colors for the font and outline.

LOOK FOR TIMING OPPORTUNITIES IN THE BACKGROUND ACTION

If your titles don't need to follow strict time restraints, look for cues in the action onscreen for your titles' entrances and exits.

In this example the seagull turns its head toward the title. Rather than have the title leave after the bird turns its head, it's more fun to have the bird look just as the title begins its exit, as if the bird notices the title sneaking away. Whatever the hypothetical scenario, seize timing opportunities whenever possible.

DESIGN LIST TEXT FOR A TRAINING VIDEO

For this project we'll design a list title for a training video. The same design can be used for other lists throughout the project with subtle variations as needed.

✔ This is a training video for home landscape projects.

✔ The overall feel is fun, organic, and noninstitutional.

✔ The title is a list of gardening secrets.

✔ This is a training DVD, so it will be played on televisions, computers, or portable DVD players.

✔ The movement of the background for this list is a dolly out (pull out) from a close-up of a flower to a wide shot that includes a background fence and greenery.

✔ The canvas is very textured and busy with flowers, and a fence, and greenery (oh my). The list will definitely need some kind of backing element between the text and the background.

✔ The layout is pretty symmetrical and has a diagonal direction.

✔ The color scheme is limited and contains a lot of white and green. Green is the dominant color, and yellow is the highlight.

✔ The titles need to stay onscreen long enough to read the whole list and end before the end of the shot. Since the shot is longer than needed, the list text won't be rushed.

Now that you have the lay of the landscape (pun intended again), let's start designing the list.

DETERMINE THE TITLE LAYOUT

Before you begin building your title, it's important to determine where you want the title to go. This image is busier on the left side than the right. The large diagonal patch of green would make an interesting place for the text. Since the design is symmetrical, it would be even better if the list could somehow follow the same diagonal pattern. Let's put the list header in the upper right of the screen where the fence meets the greenery. Then we can create the list over the greenery in size order from the shortest words to the longest. If the list is right justified, it should form a diagonal wedge shape similar to the greenery! Now that we have a plan for the layout, we need to pick the font.

SELECT A FONT AND TEST IT IN BLACK AND WHITE

Select a font that works well with this project, and then test the name of the list (Gardening Secrets) in both black and white over the background. Since the background is textured and contains dark and light elements, let's go ahead and add a classic drop shadow (030) to the black and white text. Use a white shadow for the black text and a black shadow for the white text. Create a text object with the words Gardening Secrets. Choose on organic feeling, easy to read font. I selected the Marker Felt font because it serves the purpose and has a nice handwritten feel. Duplicate the text and change it to the opposite colors of the first text.

Let's place the solo title in the corner pocket (003) aligned to the upper-right corner (inside the title safe zone). Play the video and see how the titles stand out over the background.

The black text looks better over the white part of the background, and the white text works better over the darker green areas. Let's find something that works over both areas. Also, it's clear from this text that a drop shadow alone isn't going to be enough to distinguish the text. We'll need to add an outline as well. But first, go ahead and delete the duplicate text.

MIX AND MATCH THE DOMINANT AND HIGHLIGHT COLORS IN THE TEXT

Add a dramatic (041) or heavy (042) outline and classic (030) drop shadow with a 3–5 distance to the text. Then alternate using the dominant and highlight colors for the outline and text. Use a dark green from the image for the drop shadow.

What do you think? The orange/yellow text with the dark green outline has my vote. It's easy to see and really accents the highlight color in the flowers nicely.

SOFTEN OR COVER THE BACKGROUND AS NEEDED

Although the text header looks pretty good, it will still be hard to see the list items unless the greenery in the background is less prominent. Generally, in these situations, you have three choices: crop the busy background, cover the background with a graphic, or blur the background. In this project it is important that the greenery remains, so cropping (or pruning) is not an option.

You could make a shape that fits over the greenery, color it the same as the greenery, and lower the opacity a bit to block the heavy texture of the leaves.

The downside of using that technique is that it looks like you are trying to cover up the greenery.

You could add the shape, lower the opacity, and feather the shape so it blends better.

This isn't bad, but it still looks like you're covering up something.

Try doubling the background video, creating a mask, and adding a Gaussian blur to the greenery so it is softer and less focused.

That'll work for this list. Now there's a smoother place to add the text.

BUILD THE ENTIRE LIST

Usually, list text builds one item at a time. It's a good idea to lay out the entire list first to make sure the placement and alignment is correct. Then duplicate the text object and crop or delete the words as needed to animate them in one at a time.

Keep in mind that you're aiming for the diagonal/wedge-shaped text for the list.

Create a text object with the words: Sun, Water, Fertilizer, Weekly Weeding. Add bullets (see Appendix) at the end of each item in the list since you'll be justifying it to the right. Align the text to the right and place it over the blurred background.

NOTE: I lightened the yellow color of the text and used a yellow drop shadow to help it stand out better over the dark green background and to vary the list text from the list header. Feel free to modify the text colors to taste after you have finished the alignment.

Play the video to see how the list works over the entire shot from beginning to ending. Also, make sure the list text is within the title safe boundary.

DUPLICATE THE LIST AND CROP UNNEEDED ITEMS

Next, you need to duplicate the list text as many times as there are items in the list. Put the duplicates in order in the timeline of your editing software. Then open each duplicate starting with the first one and crop out all but the first item in the list. Open the second list object and crop out all but the first two items in the list. Open the third list object and crop only the last item in the list. Leave the fourth list object as is because it contains the final list.

ANIMATE THE LIST WITH FADES OR DISSOLVES

If you used the duplicating technique described in the preceding section, you can simply add prebuilt cross dissolves between the text objects to complete the animation. The dissolves can be as long or short as you'd like. If a narrator is reading the text, try to match the pace of his or her voice. Otherwise, adjust the dissolves to taste. When in doubt, use a classic dissolve (077). The new information will dissolve in while the other items in the list appear unchanged.

That's a wrap on that title design.

DESIGN BLOCK TEXT AND KEY INFORMATION TITLES FOR A PSA

Block text can be really easy or very challenging depending on the situation. If you're creating a block that is fine-print legalese for a commercial, you don't have to worry about people reading it. You simply have to make it look like a fine-print paragraph from a document and place it somewhere onscreen for a few seconds.

In this project your job is to add a paragraph of information to a 30 second Public Service Announcement (PSA).

✔ This project is a 30 second PSA to raise public awareness about falling trees.

✔ The theme is that nature is pretty and powerful, and people aren't aware of how fragile it is. The job of this PSA is to inform the audience and give people something to think about without being pushy, preachy, or a turnoff.

✔ The goal is to deliver a paragraph of block text plus two pieces of key information text. How the paragraph and key information is delivered is not specific. As a title designer, your job is to get that text onscreen as a block or a word at a time, whichever is the most effective.

✔ This PSA will be seen on television and possibly in movie theaters along with the commercials.

✔ The movement of the background is all over the place with lots of moving shots of the forest and trees including physical camera movement such as tilts, pans, handheld, and dolly shots.

✔ The canvas is mixed, but most of the shots are fairly busy to chaotic. We probably won't need a solid backing but will definitely need an outline for the text.

✔ In this case the composition is based more on the content than any layout plan. Each shot includes giant redwoods and other forest trees. If anything, a lot of vertical lines are evident because of the trees. No composition convention is apparent in this overall piece.

✔ The color scheme is multicolored with many shades of green and brown. The color varies from shot to shot. A clear dominant or highlight color is not obvious.

✔ The titles can be onscreen for any given length of time as long as all of the text is finished at the end of the 30 seconds.

CHOOSE A FONT

Text blocks are perceived very much the same way that printed text is perceived. They are almost always serifed or sans serifed fonts because they are the easiest to read. Sans serifed fonts are more contemporary and casual. Serifed fonts feel more like newsprint or book print. Since this text contains serious information that needs to read and feel as authentic as newsworthy material, using a serifed font is a good idea. I selected the font Palatino.

CREATE THE TEXT BLOCK

Creating text blocks that you really want people to read is much more challenging than creating text to simply fulfill a legal obligation. You need to compel them to read without cluttering the screen or annoying them so much that they turn the channel.

Start by either copying and pasting the text from a word processor or typing it manually. Once you have created the initial text object, you can plan the layout and start testing fonts.

If you'd like to follow along, you'll need to type the following into a single text object: *If a tree falls in the forest... does it make a sound? Last year 20 million acres of forest were lost. What is the sound of a million trees falling? Is anyone listening? 1-555-555-TREE www.fallingtrees. listen*

Try making a single paragraph of the text, experimenting with justification, and splitting up the lines.

The text by itself is informative. Your job is to place it tastefully on the screen and encourage the audience to read it, and it is hoped, digest the information.

Unlike the other titles that you've been working with, you can choose the color and style of text first, and then worry about the layout. Layout isn't a big mystery in this project because there is no composition scheme to follow. The text will either end up as one paragraph or as short sentences. You can figure that out later.

TEST THE TEXT IN BLACK AND WHITE

As always, test the text over the background in both black and white to see if you prefer dark or light text, if you get any ideas for adding color, and if one option looks better than the other.

ADD A CONTRASTING OUTLINE

If straight black or white text isn't enough to stand out against the background, try adding a contrasting outline. In this case, a dramatic outline (041) would help the text stand out more against the busy background.

The outline helped narrow the black and white field. To me the white text with a black background looks a bit better and seems like it will be easier to read with a light and fluffy outline (043). The light and fluffy outline uses a heavy outline with a lot of softening or blur applied to the outline.

Design Block Text and Key Information Titles for a PSA

Test the light and fluffy outlined text over different shots to see how it holds up.

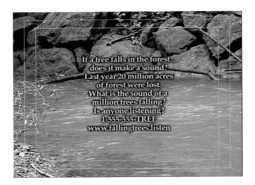 

TRY A LIGHT COLOR TO SEE IF IT MAKES A DIFFERENCE

Block text is usually white or black, but in some cases a light yellow tint can be added to help separate it from any bright white or dark black areas in the background image. The light yellow looks pretty good but not great. Chances are good that I'd stick to black and white text for this project.

EXPERIMENT WITH THE LAYOUT

Now you can continue experimenting with the layout of the text. Start with one large block of text, and then consider breaking it into smaller blocks or sentences and spacing them out through the project.

ADD SUBTLE ANIMATION, SUCH AS FADES AND DISSOLVES

Once you settle on the layout you can add fades and dissolves. If you decide to break up the text into smaller sections, try using a lingering fade or cross dissolve (079) between the text pieces to gradually fade away and introduce the next piece of text. Remember, lingering fades and cross dissolves are more polite and suggestive, and people are more likely to read the text.

KEEP AN OPEN MIND

Inspiration comes when you least expect it. Keep an open mind when you're designing text. Sometimes you'll get an idea that is really worth trying. Remember, you can always save a duplicate copy of the project and try the new text design on the copy. The best part is at the end of the day you'll have more than one version to show your client, or review yourself.

For this project I was satisfied with the text in small pieces with lingering fades and a fluffy outline... until I got another idea. What if the text didn't display over the picture at all? What if the image had a widescreen matte with black bars at the top and bottom. Then the text could go directly beneath the image. It would feel like a subtitle. People read subtitles, even if they try not to. The inspiration seemed worth a try.

Last year 20 million acres of forest were lost

What is the sound of a million trees falling?

Keeping an open mind paid off in this project because the result looks much better and cleaner, and will have a greater impact on the audience. Don't worry, I kept the lingering fades between the lines of text. I need to be sure the audience will read the text.

Is anyone listening?

1-555-555-TREE

www.fallingtrees.listen

At the end I used faster fades for the key information text because by then the audience was either looking for more information, or not.

DESIGN MAIN TITLES, CREDITS, AND INTELLECTUAL PROPERTY RIGHTS TITLES FOR A VIDEO PODCAST

The final project is to create text for a future video podcast. This is a new format that is growing rapidly, so it's good to be prepared for the latest media technology.

Titles from an actual podcast streaming on iTunes

✔ This project is a video podcast of the *Title Design Essentials* book. (Okay, this doesn't exist, but it's more realistic than *Title Design Essentials* the movie.)

✔ The feel is upbeat but still educational.

✔ This project needs a simple main title, a credit, and an intellectual property rights title (copyright).

✔ The project will be seen on computers and very small screens on portable media players.

✔ The background doesn't contain much movement, just a little shimmering and slight movement of the shapes in the corners.

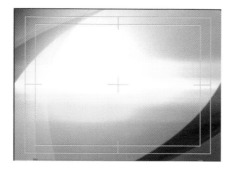

✔ The canvas is very clean, so the text won't need any shadow or outline.

✔ The background layout is fairly symmetrical with balanced angles on opposite corners.

✔ The background is monochromatic yellow.

✔ The opening titles should only last 10–15 seconds.

NOTE: The titles in the examples in this section were created in LiveType, and I left the safe zones, alignment crosshairs, and blue text base line visible for these screens so you could see the layout tools in action.

TYPE THE TITLE AND TEST IT IN BLACK AND WHITE

By now, the methodology of testing your titles in black and white should be your first step in any project.

EXPERIMENT WITH DIFFERENT LAYOUTS AND TEXT SIZES

I decided to use the Copperplate font, which uses all capital letters. I also used the pyramid main title technique (006) to stack and center the title using two different sizes of text. The size of the text should be large and easy to read on a very small screen.

ADD ANIMATION TO TASTE

The titles work fine as is, the simpler the better, so an easy fade in/fade out on the text will work. Since there is a limited amount of time for the intro to display onscreen, a fast fade (080) would be even better.

USE THE SAME FONT COLOR AND LAYOUT SCHEME
ON THE OTHER TITLES

When you're ready to create the next title, use the same font, color, and layout scheme (pyramid technique) but vary the placement of the text. In this case the author title fit well as a corner pocket credit (003), and the copyright text fit nicely in the opposite corner.

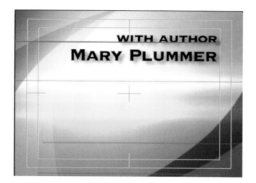 

TIP: When you are creating titles for a podcast, be sure to look at them at a size that is similar to the size of the screen they will actually be viewed on. If you can easily read the titles in a small frame size, the audience will be able to read them too.

Appendix

This appendix includes a conversion table for Roman numerals, as well as the keystrokes for symbols commonly used in titles, from trademark and copyright symbols to cents, degrees, and accent marks.

ROMAN NUMERALS	
Symbol Capitalized/Lowercase	Value
I or	1 (one)
II or ii	2 (two)
III or iii or iij	3 (three)
IV or iv or IIII or iiii	4 (four)
V or v	5 (five)
VI or vi	6 (six)
VII or vii	7 (seven)
VIII or viii	8 (eight)
IX or ix	9 (nine)
X or x	10 (ten)
L or l	50 (fifty)
C or c	100 (one hundred)
D or d	500 (five hundred)
M or m	1000 (one thousand)

Applying Symbols to Titles

Symbols can be accessed using different keystrokes or methods depending on the software and computer platform that you are using. The following table shows the keystrokes that *should* work for any of your titling applications.

If any of these keystrokes do not work for the symbol you are trying to type, check the documentation for your specific software application to determine the correct keystrokes.

NOTE: The Option key on a Macintosh keyboard is the same as the Alt key on a Windows keyboard. If you are using a third-party keyboard with a Macintosh computer, substitute the Alt key for Option key.

SYMBOLS (MACINTOSH)		
Symbol	Description	Keystrokes (Press Option and key at the same time)
™	Trademark	Option-2
©	Copyright	Option-g
®	Registered	Option-r
°	Degrees	Option-0 (zero)
•	Bullet/list dot	Option-8
¡	Upside-down exclamation mark	Option-!
¿	Upside-down question mark	Shift-Option-?

NOTE: Windows computers require the use of the numeric keypad with Num Lock active to use the numbered codes for inserting symbols, foreign characters, or accented letters. Turn on Num Lock, and then place the cursor where you want to insert the symbol or special character. Press and hold the Alt key while typing the numeric code for each symbol. There are also other methods for accessing symbols on Windows computers depending on the software that you are using.

SYMBOLS (WINDOWS)		
Symbol	Description	Keystrokes (Use numeric keypad to enter code)
™	Trademark	Alt-0153
©	Copyright	Alt-0169
®	Registered	Alt-0174
°	Degrees	Alt-0176
•	Bullet/list dot	Alt-0149
¡	Upside-down exclamation mark	Alt-0161
¿	Upside-down question mark	Alt-0191

FOREIGN CURRENCY (MACINTOSH)		
Symbol	Description	Keystrokes
€	Euro currency	Shift-Option-2
£	British Pound	Option-3
¥	Japanese Yen	Option-y
¢	Cent sign	Option-4

FOREIGN CURRENCY (WINDOWS)		
Symbol	Description	Keystrokes (Use numeric keypad to enter code)
€	Euro currency	Alt-0128
£	British Pound	Alt-0163
¥	Japanese Yen	Alt-0165
¢	Cent sign	Alt-0162

ACCENTED LETTERS (MACINTOSH)		
Symbol	Keystrokes	
Tilde ~	Option-n then type letter	Ãã, Ññ,Õõ
Acute ´	Option-e then type letter	Áá,Éé,Íí,Óó,Úú
Circumflex ^	Option- i then type letter	Ââ,Êê,Îî,Ôô,Ûû
Grave `	Option- ` then type letter	Àà, Èè,Ìì,Ò ò,Ùù
Umlaut ¨	Option- u then type letter	Ää,Ëë,Ïï,Öö,Üü,Ÿÿ

ACCENTED LETTERS (WINDOWS)			
Symbol	Keystrokes	Symbol	Keystrokes
Tilde ~	**Alt-plus number code**	**Grave `**	**Alt-plus number code**
Ã 0195	ã 0227	À 0192	à 0224
Ñ 0209	ñ 0241	È 0200	è 0232
Õ 0213	õ 0245	Ì 0204	ì 0236
Acute ´	**Alt-plus number code**	Ò 0210	ò 0242
Á 0193	á 0225	Ù 0217	ù 0249
É 0201	é 0233	**Umlaut ¨**	**Alt-plus number code**
Í 0205	í 0237	Ä 0196	ä 0228
Ó 0211	ó 0243	Ë 0203	ë 0235
Ú 0218	ú 0250	Ï 0207	ï 0235
Circumflex ^	**Alt-plus number code**	Ö 0214	ö 0246
Â 0194	â 0226	Ü 0220	ü 0252
Ê 0202	ê 0234	Ÿ 0159	ÿ 0255
Î 0206	î 0238		
Ô 0212	ô 0244		
Û 0219	û 0251		

Index